Set design by Keith E. Mitchell   Photo by Henry DiRocco

Melody Butiu and Gregory Itzin in the South Coast Repertory
production of *Shipwrecked! An Entertainment — The Amazing
Adventures of Louis de Rougemont (as Told by Himself)*.

SHIPWRECKED!
AN ENTERTAINMENT
THE AMAZING ADVENTURES
OF LOUIS DE ROUGEMONT
(AS TOLD BY HIMSELF)

BY DONALD MARGULIES

★

DRAMATISTS
PLAY SERVICE
INC.

SHIPWRECKED! AN ENTERTAINMENT — THE AMAZING ADVENTURES
OF LOUIS DE ROUGEMONT (AS TOLD BY HIMSELF)
Copyyright © 2009, Donald Margulies

All Rights Reserved

For my son, Miles

NOTES ABOUT THE PLAY

Shipwrecked! An Entertainment — The Amazing Adventures of Louis de Rougemont (As Told by Himself) is the deliberately hyperbolic title of a play about the very nature of artifice and storytelling. Intended as a celebration of theater, its presentation should be alternately thrilling and cheesy. The special effects should be clever, but determinedly low-tech; I want audiences to see the mechanics of theater, whether it's a puppeteer in plain sight, or an undisguised wire cable. The costuming should seem as if children raided their parents' closets for a game of dress-up.

No scenery is necessary. What scenic design there is should be minimal but elegant, the simpler the better. Scenes must flow seamlessly. The lighting design should be unsparingly gorgeous. And so should the music. Sound should be created onstage, in full view of the audience, by the actors. Avoid high-tech recorded sound and synthesized music.

If projections are used, they should not be photographic; they should look instead like 19th-century cross-hatched engravings, possibly hand-colored, and they should appear to be controlled by a lantern slide-projector.

The use of cute puppets or costumes suggestive of animals are forbidden. They would sink the play. I prefer an expressionistic — as opposed to literal — evocation of the events described.

The actor playing Louis must be charismatic, agile and utterly mutable; his age is unimportant as long as he is able to convince us he is an old man one minute, and a boy the next.

The play may be performed with as few as three principal actors: One portraying Louis; a second, female actor of color and a third, male actor, dividing most of the other characters. The third actor also serves as the primary Foley artist who creates sound effects before our eyes. If a company or amateur group is blessed with a large cast and few financial constraints, roles may be distributed accordingly. Try it. See how it works. (Although I still suspect the fewer — and simpler — the better.)

Directors are urged to avoid cuteness (did I already say that?) and sentimentality at all cost. Actors mustn't resort to facile caricatures. They must keep their choices subtle and true at all times, and never condescend to their characters or to their audience.

Allusions to contemporary pop culture (i.e., references to movies, television shows, celebrities, hip-hop music, etc.) are strictly forbidden. That means no slogans on T-shirts, no cheap jokes, no pandering of any kind.

Shipwrecked! is a timeless tale and should be presented as such.

SHIPWRECKED! AN ENTERTAINMENT — THE AMAZING ADVENTURES OF LOUIS DE ROUGEMONT (AS TOLD BY HIMSELF) was commissioned by South Coast Repertory (David Emmes, Producing Artistic Director; Martin Benson, Artistic Director; Paula Tomei, Managing Director) in Costa Mesa, California, where it received its world premiere on September 23, 2007. It was directed by Bart DeLorenzo; the set design was by Keith E. Mitchell; the costume design was by Candice Cain; the lighting design was by Rand Ryan; the original music and sound design were by Steven Cahill; the shadow scenic design was by Christine Marie; the dramaturg was John Glore; the production manager was Jeff Gifford; the stage manager was Erin Nelson; and the honorary producer was Laurie Smits Staude. The cast was as follows:

LOUIS DE ROUGEMONT .... Gregory Itzin
PLAYER #1 .... Melody Butiu
PLAYER #2 .... Michael David Cassady

SHIPWRECKED! received its east coast premiere at Long Wharf Theatre (Gordon Edelstein, Artistic Director; Joan Channick, Managing Director) in New Haven, Connecticut, on February 13, 2008. It was directed by Evan Cabnet; the set design was by Lee Savage; the costume design was by Jessica Wegener; the lighting design was by Tyler Micholeau; the sound design was by Drew Levy; the movement coach was Tim Acito; the dramaturg was Katherine McGerr; and the stage manager was Bonnie Brady. The cast was as follows:

LOUIS DE ROUGEMONT .... Michael Countryman
PLAYER #1 .... Angela Lin
PLAYER #2 .... Jeff Biehl

SHIPWRECKED! was subsequently produced at the Geffen Playhouse (Gilbert Cates, Producing Director; Randall Arney, Artistic Director; Stephen Eich, Managing Director), in collaboration with South Coast Repertory, in Los Angeles, California, opening on June 25, 2008. The cast, director and design team were the same as the South Coast production, except the production stage manager was Elizabeth A. Brohm; there were some changes in text and staging.

SHIPWRECKED! received its New York premiere at Primary Stages (Casey Childs, Executive Producer; Andrew Leynse, Artistic Director; Elliot Fox, Managing Director) on February 8, 2009. It was directed by Lisa Peterson; the set design was by Neil Patel; the costume design was by Michael Krass; the lighting design was by Stephen Strawbridge; the original music and sound design were by John Gromada; and the production stage manager was Matthew Melchiorre. The cast was as follows:

LOUIS DE ROUGEMONT .... Michael Countryman
PLAYER #1 .... Donnetta Lavinia Grays
PLAYER #2 .... Jeremy Bobb

CHARACTERS

LOUIS DE ROUGEMONT

PLAYER #1 (female) contributes sound effects and portrays or gives voice to:

LOUIS' MOTHER
CAPTAIN JENSEN
YAMBA, an aborigine princess, later HIS WIFE
FITZGERALD, a magazine editor
A SOCIETY LADY
ALBERT'S MOTHER
AN OCTOPUS EXPERT
A MAP MAKER
A REPORTER
A LIBRARIAN

PLAYER #2 (male) contributes sound effects and portrays or gives voice to:

A BARKEEP
BRUNO, a dog
GUNDA, Yamba's father, a tribal chief
BOBO, her brother
AN AUSTRALIAN PROSPECTOR
A SOCIETY LADY
ALBERT, a boy
QUEEN VICTORIA, a queen
A TURTLE EXPERT
A WOMBAT EXPERT
DR. LEOPOLD, an alienist
A PICKPOCKET
A NEWSBOY
A REPORTER
A LAWYER

VARIOUS PEDESTRIANS, SHIPMATES, PEARL-FISHERS, CHILDREN, PEDDLERS, PROSPECTORS, TRIBESMEN and WOMEN, SPECTATORS, THE ROYAL GEOGRAPHIC SOCIETY and HECKLERS

This play was inspired by *The Adventures of Louis de Rougemont*, a publishing sensation in England at the close of the nineteenth century. The chapter on de Rougemont in Sarah Burton's book *Impostors* (Viking, 2000) and *The Most Amazing Story a Man Ever Lived to Tell* (Angus & Robertson, 1977) by Geoffrey Maslen were invaluable resources.

SHIPWRECKED! AN ENTERTAINMENT
THE AMAZING ADVENTURES OF
LOUIS DE ROUGEMONT
(AS TOLD BY HIMSELF)

A ghost light stands in the middle of a bare stage. With the house lights still on, Louis de Rougemont, a proud, ancient man, emerges from the darkness, and looks out over the audience.

LOUIS. *(To us.)* Well well well!
Look at all you lovely-looking people out there!
My! So many of you!
(To others; surprised.) Oh! There, too!
Greetings!
You vital, hummingbird-hearted creatures!
Hello and welcome to this temple of the imagination!
This hallowed hall where stories are told!
The managers of this reputable establishment have kindly lent me use of their stage for ninety minutes or thereabouts, so that I may present to you … An Entertainment!
Allow me to introduce myself:
My name, dear audience, is Louis de Rougemont.
(To an audience member.) Aren't you clever, you're quite right, it *is* French.
Rouge meaning "red" and *mont:* "mountain."
Louis of the Red Mountain, at your service! *(He bows.)*
Are you ready to be astonished?
(He coaxes a response from the audience.) Are you? Well, good! You've come to the right place! *(Louis gestures offstage. The Players appear. He takes a note from his pocket.)*
My assistants at today's proceedings … *(Refers to the note.)* Miss _____ and Mr. _____ *[actual names of actors]. (The Players acknowledge Louis and the audience, then stand aside. They will assume all the other roles.)*

First, the law mandates that I deal with a bit of unpleasant business: Should unforeseen events occur — fire or flood — please note points of egress at the front and rear of the auditorium.

Next, you must put away any and all distracting devices and lozenges.

Go on — you know who you are.

We shall wait.

Tuck them away or we will *take* them away.

And crush them.

I am quite serious: we have specially trained people standing by. With mallets. *(He chuckles.)*

Hush, now! For I am about to tell you a story.

A fantastic and *amazing* story!

A story all the more remarkable because every word of it is true. That's right. Every word.

How do I know?

Because I lived it, dear ones.

(With a flourish.) Gentle boys and girls, kind men and ladies:

The Amazing Adventures of Louis de Rougemont! As told by himself! *(Player #1 cranks on a gramophone. The crackling recording of a fanfare is heard. The Players and stagehands wheel on racks of clothing, props, steamer trunks. Louis announces each chapter.)*

Chapter One. In which the seeds of adventure are sown.

I am born — in Paris — to parents of Swiss extraction.

My early years are spent in London, in the island-country known as the United Kingdom.

It is there where my story begins, a long, long time ago ... in the year 1860. *(He wraps himself in a blanket.)*

I am a sickly child of eight, a pale and pasty-faced boy, prone to coughs and sneezes. *(He sneezes and clutches a stuffed animal, a dog.)*

While other little children frolic in the out-of-doors, I am confined to my little bed in my little blue room. *(Children sing and play in the distance.)*

CHILDREN'S VOICES. — Ring around the rosey ...

— Come out, come out, wherever you are!

— Olly olly oxen free! *(Etc.)*

LOUIS. I can see them from my window, playing in the sun!

Oh how I long to be with them!

(To his mother.) Mother, why must I stay indoors?

Why can't I go out and play?

MOTHER. Dear child, you're a fragile boy with a delicate constitution. Exposure to heaven-knows-what nastiness lurks out there in the world would only bring harm. Best to stay indoors, darling boy. Where Mother can protect you. *(Mother hums her theme, a haunting lullaby.)*

LOUIS. *(To us.)* Father, incidentally, doesn't figure in my story; he is largely absent, off conducting business in exotic places.

Oh, but my devoted mother is there, always, at my bedside.

She is there at nightfall to tuck me in and blow out the lamp. *(She does as he describes.)*

She is there in the morning, to let the sunlight wash over me. *(She opens curtains. Shadows of window panes fall across his bed.)*

If I should drift off for a nap in the afternoon, when I awaken, she is there then, too.

MOTHER. Hello, dearest. *(She presents him with a hot scone.)*

LOUIS. Often with the gift of a scone, fresh from the cooker.

MOTHER. Careful. *(She blows on the scone; he eats it.)*

LOUIS. *(To Mother.)* Mmm. Golden raisins! My favorite!

(To us.) Mother reads to me, constantly, for hours on end. *(She reads, sotto, from* Robinson Crusoe. *He plays with a toy boat.)*

MOTHER. "I was born in the year 1632 ... in the city of York ... of a good family ... but not of that country ... "

LOUIS. Adventure stories. Fantastic tales. The great, timeless tomes. *Arabian Nights. The Odyssey. Robinson Crusoe.* Wondrous journeys, each and every one of them.

MOTHER. *(Reads audibly.)* "After we had rowed about a league and a half ... "

LOUIS. Books break down the walls of my infirmary-prison.

MOTHER. " ... a raging wave, mountain-like, came rolling astern, and took us with such a fury, that it overset the boat at once." *(Sounds of a raging storm.)*

LOUIS. My bed becomes a raft on the rocky ocean. *(He rides waves on his bed.)*

MOTHER. "I saw the sea come after me as high as a great hill, and as furious as an enemy ... "

LOUIS. Years go by. I outgrow childish things. *(He puts his toy boat and dog into a trunk. Mother hangs laundry outside.)*

LOUIS. I am healthy, but rather pale, for my cheeks have seldom been kissed by the sun.

One day I defy my Mother and go outside. *(Louis steps out into the sun.)*

MOTHER. Louis! What are you doing?

LOUIS. *(To us.)* The sun on my face feels glorious!

MOTHER. Back to bed with you this instant!

LOUIS. No, Mother, I won't go back.

My sick-bed days have come to an end.

MOTHER. What on earth are you talking about? Come back inside, have a scone.

LOUIS. I don't want a scone.

Listen to me, Mother: I've made up my mind: I'm leaving home.

MOTHER. *(Shrieks.)* You're what?! *(She drops her laundry basket.)*

LOUIS. *(To us.)* She does not take this well.

MOTHER. *(Cries.)* You can't leave! You're still a child!

LOUIS. *(To her.)* I am not a child! I am sixteen years old! Nearly seventeen!

I long to see the things written about in books!

MOTHER. Those books! Those foolish books! They've filled your head with reckless ideas!

LOUIS. No!

They've described a world I long to see with my own eyes!

Mother, dear, you've kept me safe and made me strong.

For that I am grateful.

But now it's time to let me go and begin my life. *(A short pause.)*

MOTHER. How long will you be gone?

LOUIS. How ever long it takes a young man to find his way in the world.

And, once I do, I'll come home and tell you of my journey.

(To us.) I pack my things. *(Mother hands him a book.)*

MOTHER. Take this with you.

LOUIS. *(Reads the title.)* The Plays of Mr. William Shakespeare.

MOTHER. All you will need to know about life is between its covers.

LOUIS. Thank you. *(She takes cash from a purse.)*

MOTHER. Here, this, too.

LOUIS. Oh, no, Mother, I couldn't; it's your savings.

MOTHER. Please, son. Take it. Spend it wisely.

LOUIS. Thank you. I will.

MOTHER. Goodbye, darling boy.

LOUIS. Goodbye, Mother. *(They embrace. He starts to go.)*
MOTHER. *(Shouts, suddenly.)* Louis! *(He stops.)*
Be careful out there!
LOUIS. Worry not, Mother. Your Louis will be fine.
MOTHER. The world is a dangerous place!
LOUIS. That may be so. But it's also marvelous! *(He waves goodbye as his mother recedes, humming her lullaby. To us:)* And so I enter … the real world! *(The song is lost in a cacophony of city sounds and the bustle of the marketplace.)*
VARIOUS PEDDLERS. Chickens! Pigs! Potatoes! Geese! *(Etc. Louis is jostled by pedestrians.)*
A PEDESTRIAN. Hey! Watch where you're walking!
LOUIS. Sorry.
ANOTHER PEDESTRIAN. What're you, blind?
LOUIS. So sorry. *(A Pickpocket bumps into him.)*
PICKPOCKET. I beg your pardon, sir!
LOUIS. No, I beg *your* pardon. *(The Pickpocket goes; Louis realizes his pocket has been picked.)*
LOUIS. Oh, no! Mother's savings! I've been robbed! *(Shouts.)* Thief! Come back here! *(To us.)* My first night of freedom and I am penniless!
Tossed about on the rough streets of London.
Lonely. Desperate. *(To the heavens.)* What more could possibly go wrong?!
(Thunder! Lightning! Rain! Louis puts up his collar.)
My clothes are drenched to the skin.
I am cold and wet and miserable. *(He sneezes.)*
What ever made me think I could survive in the world?
It was hubris! Sheer and utter folly!
I find shelter from the rain in a darkened doorway when a certain gentleman — *(A Barkeep evicts a rowdy patron, Captain Jensen.)*
BARKEEP. Get out!
CAPTAIN JENSEN. Get yer bloody, stinkin' hands offa me! *(Freeze.)*
LOUIS. — well, there is nothing "gentle" about him, really … *(Unfreeze.)*
BARKEEP. And stay out, you drunken old sea dog!
CAPTAIN JENSEN. Who you callin' a drunken old sea dog? I ain't no dog! The name is Jensen! Captain Peter Jensen! An' if you don't like it, you can blow it out your —
LOUIS. *(To the captain.)* Sir! Excuse me. Are you alright?

15

CAPTAIN JENSEN. *(Startled.)* What? Who's there? Who said that?

LOUIS. I did, sir. Over here.

CAPTAIN JENSEN. Who are you?

LOUIS. Fear not, sir. My name is Louis de Rougemont.

I mean you no harm.

I couldn't help but overhear you.

Did you say you are a sea captain?

CAPTAIN JENSEN. Indeed I am!

LOUIS. Of a ship of your own?

CAPTAIN JENSEN. I should say! What kind of captain would I be without a ship o' me own? I'd 'ave no business callin' meself a captain, now would I!

LOUIS. Well, no, I suppose not. What's it called, your ship?

CAPTAIN JENSEN. She's called … *The Wonder World!* (A tinkle of wind chimes.)

LOUIS. *The Wonder World!* What a wonderful name for a ship!

CAPTAIN JENSEN. Mm. She's a good gal, she is. Forty tons and sturdy as a boulder. To think I'll be back at her helm in just two days' time!

LOUIS. In two days' time did you say?! What happens in two days' time?

CAPTAIN JENSEN. I depart on me next sea-farin' journey, that's what.

LOUIS. *(To us.)* An adventure! *(To the captain.)* Oh, sir, I envy you so! ⟶ why? — but an inkling + listen

Why, ever since I was a little boy tucked in my little bed I dreamt of sailing!

CAPTAIN JENSEN. Aw, in yer little bed, isn't that sweet. Well, fancy that. I just so 'appen to 'ave room on board for another shipman.

LOUIS. Room on board?! For another shipman?!

CAPTAIN JENSEN. You wouldn't be interested in *joinin'* me on this expedition by any chance, now, would ya?

LOUIS. Joining you on this expedition?!

CAPTAIN JENSEN. Are you gonna repeat every last bloody thin' I say?

LOUIS. No, sir. Sorry, sir.

What sort of expedition is it?

CAPTAIN JENSEN. A pearlin' expedition!

LOUIS. A pearlin' expedition?!

CAPTAIN JENSEN. Didn't I tell ya, stop repeatin' every bloomin' thin' I say!

LOUIS. *(Overlap.)* I'm sorry, I'm sorry. Where are these pearls?

CAPTAIN JENSEN. Far away from 'ere, lad, that's for sure. 'Alfway 'round the world. On the far side of the globe.

LOUIS. Where, exactly?

CAPTAIN JENSEN. The Coral Sea!

LOUIS. The Coral Sea?! —

CAPTAIN JENSEN. Hey!

LOUIS. Sorry. I mean, where *is* the Coral Sea?

CAPTAIN JENSEN. Australia! *(A map of Australia unfurls. Captain Jensen uses a pointer.)* 'Ere, all along the Great Barrier Reef, miles and miles of precious pearls slumber in their shells waitin' for some lucky bloke to come along and *snatch* 'em from the deep!

LOUIS. Who?

CAPTAIN JENSEN. You're lookin' at 'im! *(He laughs coarsely.)* So ya comin' with me or ain't ya?

LOUIS. *(To us.)* What happens next, dear audience, I think you can guess. *(Transition.)*

Chapter Two. In which my fateful journey begins.

The day of departure.

There she is: *The Wonder World!* My, she's a beauty!

Expert pearl-divers from Malaysia, thirty or more, make up the crew.

Suddenly, out of nowhere, a four-legged creature of the most ungainly sort — a preposterous canine of the mongrel variety — knocks me to the deck and slathers my face with kisses. *(Bruno the Dog does just that.)*

CAPTAIN JENSEN. *(Gruffly.)* Bruno! Get yer 'airy rump over 'ere! *(Bruno reluctantly goes to his master, but pines for Louis.)*

LOUIS. Bruno, the captain's dog, is to accompany us on our expedition.

Of all the men boarding this ship, he's singled me out as his new best friend.

It is devotion at first sight.

And I must say, the feeling is mutual. *(Louis and Bruno exchange a fond glance. Transition.)*

The Wonder World sets sail!

Goodbye! Goodbye, England! Fare thee well!

Look at me! I am a sailor!

Wind in my hair, salt on my skin.

A man of the world at last!

Everything is just as I dreamt it would be!

Everything, that is, until our very first night at sea. *(The boat rocks back and forth. He gets queasy.)*

Oh, dear.

It was always smooth sailing in my dreams. The ship rides the waves and plunges. Rides and plunges. Rises and smacks and climbs and tumbles. *(He throws up.)*

The seasickness lasts a few wretched days.

When suddenly it lifts! Like a fever.

Once I find my sea legs, the journey looks so much brighter!

Silvery dolphins escort us on either side, racing and leaping into the air as our ship slices through the water. *(Bruno barks at the dolphins.)*

We catch bluefish and snapper and fry them and eat together, all of us, the captain, the crew, Bruno and me.

We sing, like children. *(The crew sings a shanty; Louis joins in.)*

We sail merrily in this fashion for weeks.

Until. One lazy afternoon …

While the Captain sleeps off his consumption of rum … *(Captain Jensen collapses and snores.)*

The men are out in boats casting nets for our next meal. Bruno and I sit on the deck.

(To Bruno.) Bruno, this is where I belong!

Where I've always meant to be! *(To us.)* Suddenly, piercing the sunny tranquility of the day …

A sea monster rises from the deep! *(Ominous music. The shadow of an octopus appears.)*

An octopus! A giant octopus sets its sights on a lone, unsuspecting fisherman! *(Bruno barks.)*

I am struck dumb!

I want to shout, "Look! Behind you!

You're about to be snatched by an octopus!"

But instead I say *(Attempts to make sounds.)*

The poor pearl fisher is taken utterly by surprise.

PEARL-FISHER. Help! Helllppp!!!

LOUIS. Hideous tentacles rise up, five, ten, fifteen feet long, like gigantic snakes from the sea, and imprison the man in a deadly embrace!

All at once, man and boat are dragged down, down to the watery depths!

PEARL FISHER. AHHHHHHHHHHHH!!!!! *(The Pearl fisher perishes.)*

LOUIS. *(Frantically.)* Captain! Captain! Wake up!

CAPTAIN JENSEN. *(Gruffly.)* What is it?

LOUIS. *(In a frantic rush of words.)* A giant octopus just burst from the sea and snatched a man and his boat and dragged them down to the depths!

CAPTAIN JENSEN. *(Overlap.)* Easy, boy, easy! Slow down!

LOUIS. It's an omen, Captain!

We've got to turn back!

CAPTAIN JENSEN. Are you out of your mind, we ain't turnin' back!

LOUIS. It's a sign, I tell you! Our mission is doomed!

CAPTAIN JENSEN. Nonsense! It's just one man's bum luck! Now I don't want to 'ear another word 'bout omens!

LOUIS. *(To us.)* But the ominous feeling lingers, for days and nights, until we drop anchor at our destination, the Coral Sea!

The pearl fishermen celebrate our arrival by leaping into the water like excited frogs! *(Pearl fishers gleefully shout and take to the water.)*

Oh, what joy!

I cannot stand here while they have all the fun! I must see what they see down below — with my own eyes!

I take a deep, deep breath — the deepest I can take — and ... *(Splash! He is underwater. Awestruck:)* Oh my heavens!

It is a magical world down below!

A watery wonderland!

Oh, look! An underwater forest!

Tall sea grasses, as tall as a man, wave to and fro in the current.

Clusters of coral rise from the bottom of the sea, spectacularly splashed with reds and greens and golds.

Gaily colored fish swim by, whole schools of them, unperturbed by the peculiar creatures in their midst.

This is the wonder I dreamt of, tucked inside my little bed in my little blue room!

This enchanted place. God's aquarium! *(Transition.)*

Chapter Three. In which unforeseen events occur.

The pearl harvest is underway.

Day after day the men dive in, snatch oysters from the watery floor and, minutes later, burst to the surface brown and shiny and gulping for air.

The captain and I shuck open shell after shell.

Inside each oyster shell lurks a pearl.

A perfectly formed little gem.

Perfectly smooth. Perfectly round.

Perfectly radiant.

Rose-colored, yellow, the purest of white.

Like a little moon one holds in one's hand. *(The Captain laughs greedily.)*

Captain Jensen gloats over them like a miser with his gold.

We put the pearls in, of all things, pickle jars! *(Louis examines a pearl.)*

Hm, that's odd …

(To the captain.) Look, Captain, something is wrong with this pearl.

CAPTAIN JENSEN. What's the matter with it?

LOUIS. It's entirely black. I'll just toss it back into the —

CAPTAIN JENSEN. Oh, no you don't! Give it 'ere. *(Louis does.)*

Well, I'll be! Look at that! Black as night can be! I've only 'eard 'bout these things but never laid eyes on one of 'em before.

LOUIS. You mean it's good?

CAPTAIN JENSEN. Good?! Is it good?! Yes, you fool! Yes, it's good! Black pearls are the rarest, most precious pearls of all!

LOUIS. *(To us.)* I had no idea!

CAPTAIN JENSEN. Why, this one pearl, this one little pearl is worth more than all the others put together! If there's *one* in these waters, there must be many more! *(To the crew.)* Men! Get back down there! All of ye! Bring up every last oyster shell you can find!

LOUIS. The Captain is driven mad with greed.

CAPTAIN JENSEN. We will scour the ocean floor!

LOUIS. He is a man possessed, stricken with "pearl fever."

CAPTAIN JENSEN. *(To a pearl-fisher.)* As long as there's a shell to be snatched, we will not rest! *(Wind. Rumbles of thunder.)*

LOUIS. He pays no mind to the gathering storm. *(To the captain.)* Captain! Look! A monsoon is brewing!

CAPTAIN JENSEN. It's nothing, it'll pass! Keep shuckin' those shells!

LOUIS. *(To us.)* The sky takes on a dull, strange, colorless hue.

The clouds grow ever more sinister. *(To Captain Jensen.)* Captain, look at the sky! See how dark it's become?!

CAPTAIN JENSEN. Pay it no mind! A minor squall!

LOUIS. If we raise anchor now we could try to beat the storm!

CAPTAIN JENSEN. Nonsense! We're stayin' put!

LOUIS. But, Captain —

CAPTAIN JENSEN. You will do as I say! Keep shuckin'!

LOUIS. *(To us.)* I follow his orders because he is my captain but in my heart I know he is making a dreadful mistake. *(More thunder. Lightning.)*

CAPTAIN JENSEN. The pearls, Louis! Tend to the pearls!

LOUIS. But Captain, the waves are getting higher!

CAPTAIN JENSEN. We'll take a bit of water at most! Keep shuckin'! *(The storm intensifies. They must shout to be heard.)*

LOUIS. *(Shouts, to the captain.)* CAPTAIN, I IMPLORE YOU!
    I FEAR FOR OUR SAFETY AND THAT OF OUR CREW!
    WHAT GOOD ARE PEARLS IF WE LOSE OUR LIVES?!
    WE CAN'T TRADE PEARLS IN HEAVEN! *(The weather becomes a tempest that tosses them and the boat about.)*

CAPTAIN JENSEN. MARK MY WORDS! IT'LL SOON BLOW OVER! *(The tempest dies down.)*

LOUIS. *(To us.)* As quickly as the tempest builds in ferocity, it dies down to a whisper. *(A sibilant whoosh.)*

CAPTAIN JENSEN. Ha ha ha! See that? What did I tell ya? Didn't I tell you it would blow over! Huh? Didn't I?

LOUIS. *(To Captain Jensen, over "Huh?")* Yes, sir. Yes, you did, you certainly did.

CAPTAIN JENSEN. You little worry wart, you!

LOUIS. That I am. I am a worry wart.

CAPTAIN JENSEN. *(Teasing.)* Worry wart, worry wart! *(They laugh in relief. Bruno, sensing danger, howls.)*

LOUIS. *(To Bruno.)* Bruno? What is it, boy? What's wrong? *(Weather sounds build.)*

I see the source of his distress.

The calm, shiny surface of the sea ripples, ever so gently.

As if a rock were tossed into the water, somewhere, miles away, and the echoing ripples have only now found us.

I realize we're turning, the ship is moving, turning itself around, barely perceptibly at first, then ever more emphatically, until we spin completely around, over and over. Like an out-of-control merry-go-round, faster and faster!

(Shouts, to him.) WHAT IS IT, CAPTAIN? WHAT'S HAP-PENING?

CAPTAIN JENSEN. WE'RE CAUGHT IN THE EYE OF A WHIRLPOOL!

LOUIS. WHAT?

CAPTAIN JENSEN. A WHIRLPOOL!!!

LOUIS. *(To us.)* Spinning, whirling, spiraling downward we go, into a watery void!

Storm clouds rumble angrily and collide with one another! *(Crashes of thunder. Bolts of lightning. Torrential rain. More dramatic than ever before.)*

The heavens crack open with blue-white light!

Hurricane winds whip our sails!

And water — sheets of it — spills down from the sky!

Then, like a spectacular monster from the sea, a wave, like no wave I have ever seen or even dared to imagine, rises out of the water like a massive wall of brick, races toward us like a runaway fortress, and *smacks* into our ship! *(Smack! They shout as the ship is rocked.)*

LOUIS and CAPTAIN JENSEN. AHHHH!!!!

LOUIS. *(To us.)* The captain is tossed overboard!

(To Captain Jensen, shouting.) CAPTAIN! TAKE MY HAND!

CAPTAIN JENSEN. NEVER MIND ME! EVERY MAN FOR HIMSELF!

LOUIS. CAPTAIN, DON'T LEAVE ME!

CAPTAIN JENSEN. GOODBYE, LOUIS! GOD BE WITH YOU! *(Captain Jensen is washed away.)*

LOUIS. CAPTAIN!! COME BACK!

(To us.) The sea lashes at our hobbled ship without mercy!

The cascades of water are so thick I cannot see!

(Calls.) BRUNO?!! BRUNO, WHERE ARE YOU?!!! *(To us.)* Oh, no! Is my dear canine friend lost in the cataclysm?

The wind roars like an angry lion!

The wooden mast above me creaks and moans with every blast of fury.

It blows so hard I cannot stand.

I crawl on the deck and clutch whatever solid thing is within reach.

The moaning mast snaps like a twig and comes crashing down!

(Snap! Crack! Clunk!)

I am knocked unconscious! *(He collapses. Transition. Silence.)*

The storm passes.

A terrible calm descends.

I know not how long I slumber.

I am awakened by a strange, yet familiar, slurping sensation. *(Bruno licks his face. To Bruno:)* Bruno! Bruno, you made it!

Thank God you made it! *(To us.)* We cling to one another on the floating wreckage.

There is not a cloud in the blue, blue sky.

It's as if the tempest had never taken place, that it was all a miserable dream.

I survey the vast blueness and see … Nothing.

Absolutely nothing.

No capsized fishing boats.

No sign of my shipmates.

No Captain Jensen. No one at all.

(Calling out from the wreckage.) Hello? Is anyone out there?

(Sounds of gulls. To us:) I am alone. *(Bruno barks.)*

Well, not entirely. Bruno is with me, of course. *(To Bruno.)* Looks like it's just you and me, boy. Just you and me. *(Transition.)*

Chapter Four. In which I face an uncertain future.

Days go by. Our battered boat barely stays afloat.

Weak with thirst and hunger, I lay motionless, my skin baked and burned by the relentless sun.

My tongue: parched and swollen.

I am … delirious. *(Delirium.)* Look! A giant pink porpoise! Flying through the air!

No, not a porpoise, a strange baby whale! *(Mother, humming her lullaby, drifts across upstage but she cannot see him.)*

MOTHER. *(Sing-song, haunting, faraway.)* Louis…?

LOUIS. Who is that?

MOTHER. Where are you, Louis?

LOUIS. Mother? Mother is that you?

MOTHER. Where's my boy?

LOUIS. I'm here, Mother.

MOTHER. Come out, come out, wherever you are!

LOUIS. I'm right here, Mother! Can't you see me?

MOTHER. *(Doesn't see him.)* Why did you go, Louis? Why did you have to go so very far away?

LOUIS. I'm sorry, Mother. I wanted to see the world!

MOTHER. *(Still looking.)* Louis...? *(She disappears.)*

LOUIS. Mother! Don't go, Mother!

Please! Take me with you! I want to go home!

(He cries. To us:) Oh, how I wish I were an untroubled little boy again, my mother at my bedside reading me adventure tales.

Fabulous stories that all somehow end happily, with daring rescues and tearful homecomings.

What about *my* story? Is this where it ends?

On floating wreckage in the middle of the Coral Sea?

(Bruno barks, ending the reverie. To Bruno:) What is it, boy? What's out there? *(Louis squints in the distance.)*

Something ... blurry. Green. I see green.

A reef. A little slip of land.

An island!

Bruno, it's an island! *(To us.)* I jump into the water! *(He does.)*

Bruno jumps in after me! *(Bruno follows, dog-paddling.)*

I swim but the current is strong. Too strong.

And I am too weak to swim against it.

(Louis falls back in exhaustion. Bruno barks plaintively, his paddling more furious. To Bruno:) I can't, Bruno. I can't go on.

You go. Go on. Swim ashore.

Thatta boy. Swim to safety. *(Bruno pines.)*

You did your best. Go. Let me drown.

(They enact what is described. To us, urgently:) He clenches a hank of my shirt between his teeth and tugs me through the waves! *(Bruno, teeth clenched, hauls Louis to shore.)*

Water ... Rock ... Pebbles ... Sand ...

I am ashore. On solid ground.

Saved from certain watery death by my trusted dog.

(Louis looks around with trepidation. To Bruno:) What is this place, Bruno? Where are we? *(To us.)* The gravity of my situation begins to dawn on me:

This unremarkable patch of land in the midst of blue-green nothingness ...

This sandy oasis on the far side of the world ... *(To Bruno.)* Bruno? I believe we're home. *(Transition.)*

Chapter Five. Marooned!

As if by some divine intervention, the disabled *Wonder World* beaches as well, and on it provisions that survived the storm.

Barrels of fresh water and tinned food.

Oak chests packed with blankets and medicines.

Tools and tomahawks, and bows and arrows.

A single, water-logged volume, *The Plays of Mr. William Shakespeare*, I set out in the sun to dry.

Then, mysterious glistening objects wash ashore.

What ever can they be? Jellyfish?

I approach with caution to get a better look.

(A beat.) Why, they're pickle jars!

Untouched by catastrophe, filled with rare and precious pearls!

I laugh with bitter irony. *(He laughs with bitter irony.)*

For I am rich. I have in my possession a fortune in pearls!

But what good does a fortune do me, here, in the middle of nowhere? Nothing. It means nothing! *(Transition.)*

I do not dwell very long on my depressing predicament for I have more pressing needs than wallowing in self-pity.

Namely, learning to survive. *(He finds a hand mirror in the debris.)*

With the aid of a broken looking-glass, I try to get a fire started. *(He reflects the sun in the mirror to start a fire.)*

Come on, flame, ignite!

It smolders. It catches!

Oh, blessed sight! *(The fire crackles.)*

I feed it with brush and branches and keep it burning all the time in the hope that a passing ship will see the smoke.

Nothing. *(Lights shift many times from night to day to night again.)*

The days pass.

Weeks turn into months and months into seasons.

Bruno and I become accustomed to our new home. *(Louis and Bruno huddle together under a huge moon.)*

Gradually we lose our fear of the unknown.

The strange becomes familiar.

We learn to recognize the island's sounds. *(He listens and identifies each sound.)*

Owls.

Waves.

Wombats scuttling through the trees and rising in clouds every sunset.

The sky fills with stars.

We study the stars and constellations.

(To Bruno, pointing to the sky.) Look, Bruno, Cassiopeia!

(Bruno, disinterested, scratches himself. To us:) We wait out storms huddled together in a cave.

And sing to pass the time. *(Louis sings. Bruno howls along.)*

I recite whole passages from Shakespeare: *(Falsetto.)* "O Romeo, Romeo! Wherefore art thou Romeo?

Deny thy father and refuse thy name … " *(Bruno howls.)*

For amusement, I practice my gymnastic skills. *(He demonstrates each of the following.)*

High jumps. Head stands.

Cartwheels. Somersaults.

I teach myself how to walk on stilts.

I become quite proficient at it, too, given all the free time I have to practice.

Time is a commodity of which I have plenty.

When I'm not honing my acrobatics, I play with my new friends, the giant sea turtles. *(He demonstrates on a trunk.)*

I ride them. As if they're little ponies.

I sit atop their gnarly shells, as I would upon a horse's saddle, and we glide through the water!

I devise a method of steering which consists of a gentle poke in the eye.

If I want my turtle to turn right, I poke my great toe into his left eye.

And if I wish to go left, a poke in the right.

It is so much fun!

Still, not a day goes by that I don't climb up to the highest hilltop and look all around — three hundred and sixty degrees — for a boat in the distance.

Finally, one day …

(To Bruno.) Bruno, a sail! I see a sail! *(To us.)* A ship is but a few miles away! *(Shouts, jumps, waves to the ship.)* Hello! Up here! Look! *(To us.)* In my mind, I'm already home.

Reunited with mother.

Taking a bath.

Eating scones.

But wait! Where are you going? *(To us.)* The ship doesn't stop, it keeps sailing. *(Shouts, waves to the ship.)* Stop! Come back here!

Don't you see me?! Please! Don't leave me! Come back!

NO!!! *(He and Bruno howl.)*

NOW I'LL NEVER BE RESCUED!

I'M DOOMED! DOOMED, I SAY!

DESTINED TO LIVE OUT MY DAYS ON THIS STUPID LITTLE ISLAND! *(To the heavens.)* WHY?! WHAT HAVE I DONE TO DESERVE THIS FATE?!

(He prostrates himself in despair. To us:) I fall into a very deep sleep.

A sleep wrought by weariness and the loss of all hope.

(He sleeps. Bruno watches over him, surveying the horizon. Finally, the dog sees something and barks. Drowsily:) Bruno. Please. Let me sleep. *(The barking becomes more insistent. Acquiesces.)* Alright …

(He looks out at the horizon. Stunned, he gets to his feet. To us.) Oh, my God.

Something is out there.

Some kind of boat. A catamaran of the crudest design.

And it's floating toward our shore!

(Shouts, waves.) Here! Over here! *(To us.)* We run down the hill to the beach. *(To Bruno.)* Bruno, we're saved! We're going home! *(To us.)* I run into the water and swim toward the boat.

I hoist myself aboard. *(He does. He gasps.)*

Inside lay three people.

An old man, a young woman and a boy.

Aborigines!

Displaced members of an ancient tribe.

Alive but barely conscious.

I paddle frantically to get them to dry land.

And pull them to safety, one by one.

Here, dear audience, my saga takes an unexpected turn.

For I am not rescued.

Instead I am handed a different role, that of rescuer.

Deprived of human companionship for *two and a half years* …

I am alone no more. *(Transition.)*

Chapter Six. In which my isolation ends.

My visitors are weak from exposure to the elements.

I shield them from the baking sun.

The young woman is the first to revive.

I greet her with a reassuring smile.

(To her.) Hello! *(The Young Woman screams and recoils in terror. To us:)* I frighten *her*!

It hadn't occurred to me that I could frighten anyone.

But of course! An Englishman is as exotic to an aborigine as an aborigine is to an Englishman. *(To her.)* Young lady! I mean you no harm!

In fact, I'm fairly certain I saved your life! *(To us.)* To which she replies …

YOUNG WOMAN. Aiiiiaiiiiiaiiii! WOOWOOOWOOO!

LOUIS. Her cry rouses her compatriots.

OLD MAN. WAHWAHWAHWAHWAHH!

LOUIS. *(To the Young Woman, Boy and Old Man.)* Good people, do not be afraid! I am a man of peace!

(They become more and more agitated. To us:) But that only makes matters worse.

What can I do to assuage their fears? *(Paces.)* Think, Louis. Think. Use your wits. *(A beat.)* Ah ha! I've got it! *(To us.)* I run through my entire acrobatic repertoire!

Cartwheels! Hand stands! Somersaults!

Two, three, four times! Until I drop from exhaustion. *(He frantically performs until he drops to the ground, panting.)*

They approach me with curiosity.

The old man pokes me with his foot. Ow.

The young woman kneels and offers me water.

(To her; surprised.) Thank you.

(Their eyes meet, accompanied by the pluck of a violin string. To us:) Our eyes meet. Our gazes freeze.

The gulf between our vastly different worlds instantly gets considerably smaller.

With a simple gesture of kindness, a powerful bond begins to take form. *(To her.)* I am Louis. What is your name?

YAMBA. Yamba.

LOUIS. Yamba. *(She nods. He points to himself.)* Louis.

YAMBA. Louis.

LOUIS. Yes. That's right: My name is Louis. *(To us.)* The old man, she somehow conveys, is her father.

YAMBA. Gunda.

LOUIS. *(To Gunda.)* Gunda. *(Gunda grunts.)*

LOUIS. *(To us.)* And the boy, her baby brother.

YAMBA. Bobo.

LOUIS. *(To Bobo.)* Hello, Bobo. *(Bobo does cartwheels. Louis applauds.)* Excellent, Bobo! Well done! *(To us.)* Yamba tells me her story.

YAMBA. *(Ad lib.)* Aya woo a yako moo tanaka boray anunda tali banno … *(Etc. Yamba speaks in her obscure language and uses movement to illustrate her story.)*

LOUIS. For those of you who don't speak Yamba's language, allow me to translate. *(Yamba resumes softly and pantomimes while Louis translates.)*

"Our home is far away, many suns and moons away, where we live with our people.

"We set out, as we often do, in our little boat and went from island to island to catch sea turtles.

"A terrible storm came and the wind blew us far from home.

"For days the sun baked us and we ran out of water.

"We got weaker and weaker and fell asleep.

"We were adrift until *you* came along" — meaning I —

"like a god of the ocean" — her words, not mine —

"and saved us and brought us to your home."

(To her.) This is not my home. My home, too, is far away.

(To us.) We learn to communicate. Word by word, we learn each other's language. *(To her.)* Sand.

YAMBA. Sand. Yono.

LOUIS. Yono. *(Points up.)* Sky.

YAMBA. Sky. Lahlo.

LOUIS. Lahlo.

YAMBA. *(Tracks a bird.)* Twee.

LOUIS. Twee? Bird.

YAMBA. Bird.

LOUIS. *(To us.)* We play. Like children. *(They chase one another.)* I perform magic tricks with the looking-glass.

We make a game of it. *(Louis deflects sunlight; she steps on spots of light. She grabs the mirror, sees her reflection and recoils in horror.)*

She has never seen her own reflection before. *(To her.)* Be not afraid. It's only a looking-glass.

See? That is you. That is Yamba. *(He holds it up for her to see. She conquers her fear and makes faces at herself. Yamba and Louis laugh. Bruno growls at Yamba. To Bruno:)* Bruno, no! Bad dog! Bruno, sit! Sit!

(Bruno sits, resentfully. To Yamba:) I'm so sorry. This is so unlike him.

Are you all right?

(Louis touches Yamba. Bruno snarls. To Bruno:) Bad dog! What

is the matter with you?! *(To us.)* Of course! Why didn't I think of it before?!

He's jealous! The poor dog is jealous! Of Yamba! *(To Bruno, gently.)* Here, boy. *(Bruno goes to him.)*

That's a good boy. Just because I'm spending time with someone new doesn't mean I don't care about you anymore. We can all be friends. *(Bruno licks him.)*

Yes, I love you, too. *(Louis and Yamba scratch Bruno, who rolls on his back in pleasure.)*

You're such a good boy, Bruno. Yes, you are. You're still my best friend, Bruno. My very very best in the whole wide world.

(Transition. Louis, Yamba, Gunda, Bobo and Bruno gather around a fire. To us:) Every night, we gather around the fire, like a very odd family, for something the aborigines call a carroboree. *(Gunda chants.)*

Gunda chants. We tell stories. I recite Shakespeare. *(To them.)*
" … Let me not,
Since I have my dukedom got
And pardon'd the deceiver, dwell
In this bare island by your spell;
But release me from my bands
With the help of your good hands:
Gentle breath of yours my sails
Must fill, or else my project fails,
Which was to please … "

(They applaud. Bruno howls. To us.) Weeks go by in this pleasant fashion. Until one night, Yamba points to the sky and asks:

YAMBA. *(Points.)* Do you see that star?

LOUIS. *(To us.)* Her English is perfect by now.

YAMBA. That bright, bright star on the horizon?

LOUIS. Yes, I see it.

YAMBA. There, beneath that star, that is my home.

LOUIS. You miss it, don't you?

YAMBA. Oh yes, very much.

LOUIS. It can't be very far. A few days' sailing at most.

YAMBA. If only we had a strong enough boat …

LOUIS. *(An idea.)* We'll build one!

YAMBA. Really?!

LOUIS. Between your catamaran and what we can salvage from *The Wonder World* I'm sure we could make something seaworthy.

YAMBA. You will come, too?

LOUIS. Of course I will come with you. *(Bruno barks.)*

(To Bruno.) And Bruno, too, of course! *(To her.)* Do you think for a moment I could send you off on a boat and stay behind? No, I could not.

Nothing would please me more than to shepherd you and your loved ones home.

YAMBA. Thank you, Louis! Thank you! *(She kisses his cheek, which makes him blush. She blushes, too.)*

I must go tell Papa and Bobo. *(Calls.)* Gunda-papa! Bobo! Anu toto lo manu! *(Etc. She goes. He touches his kissed cheek.)*

LOUIS. *(To us.)* Yamba's kiss reminds me of how starved for affection I have been all these years on the island.

Bruno licks me all the time, that is true, but a lick, after all, is still a lick.

I realize that the feelings I have for Yamba are unlike anything I have ever felt for another human being.

My heartbeat quickens at the very thought of her.

My palms sweat.

My head feels as if it floats above my shoulders.

The sensation is a bit like seasickness but without the vomiting.

I take note of it. *(Transition.)*

Chapter Seven. In which I prepare to leave my island home for the land of the aborigines and points unknown.

We cobble together a tight and tidy ship.

There is no room on board for my collection of pearls so I bury the jars in the sand.

This way, a fortunate prospector sometime in the future might happen upon hidden treasure.

(I have every reason to believe they are buried there still.) *(Transition.)*

Off we go!

I watch the island recede and much to my surprise …

What's this? There are tears in my eyes!

I never would have thought I'd grow attached to this curious place. Why, it feels as if I'm leaving home.

We are blessed with smooth sailing.

Not once does the wind change or the clouds threaten.

On the tenth day at sea, we cruise through chains of uninhabited islands.

A volcano rumbles.

(To them; points.) Look! A volcano!

YAMBA. We know this place! We are almost there!

LOUIS. *(To us.)* Soon, a shoreline is sighted.

And, as we get closer, figures dot the landscape. *(Tribesmen wearing war masks and armed with spears, array themselves defensively along the shore.)*

Men. Women. Children.

Armed with spears and grave expressions. *(To Yamba.)* Yamba … Your people …

Why do they look at me with such cold eyes?

YAMBA. They don't know what to make of you. They cannot tell if you are friend or foe.

LOUIS. *(To the tribe.)* Friend! I am your friend! *(The tribe grunts aggressively, scaring Louis.)*

YAMBA. Say nothing! Let Gunda speak to them.

GUNDA. Tallu anu octo tooty dunda … attu tuttoto farnu bucca … *(Continues sotto voce.)*

LOUIS. *(To us.)* He tells them how I came to their rescue "like a god of the ocean" — his words — and took them into my hut for many months and how I built the boat that made it possible for them to come home. *(The tribe grunts again.)*

But the people are unmoved.

They inspect me from head to toe. *(Members of the tribe circle, sniff, pinch, and poke at Louis.)*

(To the tribe.) Ow.

Oof.

I beg your pardon! *(They suspensefully confer among themselves.)*

(To us.) I await their verdict.

What will it be?

Torn limb from limb and roasted on a spit?

Or welcomed like a brother into the tribe? *(They continue to deliberate.)*

They take their sweet time.

I become convinced that they're discussing what wine goes best with de Rougemont.

(To himself.) Think, Louis. Act quickly.

How best to win their trust?

(Pause; an idea.) My display of acrobatics! *(Louis performs, then finishes, breathlessly. A tense silence. Finally, the group cheers.)*

(To us.) The would-be cannibals are bowled over!

I am welcomed into the tribe! Treated like royalty!

No, even greater than a king: like a divinity! *(The tribe celebrates.)*

To show their high regard, they cover my body in colored clay and give me a fantastic headdress adorned with cockatoo feathers.

Bruno, as my prized pet, is decorated also, and treated with respect, the likes of which is rarely bestowed upon a dog. *(Bruno is given a headdress to wear.)*

They sit me in a throne-like chair and the women of the tribe line up to present me with gifts.

Delicacies of all kinds.

Baskets full of bananas, pineapples, figs.

Rats, opossums.

Baked snake becomes one of my favorite dishes.

Crispy on the outside, tender and juicy on the inside.

Mm. Quite delicious.

Next, as part of my indoctrination into the tribe, I am invited to choose a bride. *(Tribeswomen line up. Louis addresses individual women.)*

No.

No, thank you.

Thank you, no.

(To us.) This is a hollow exercise. For there is no question whom I wish to be my bride. *(He turns to Yamba and gets down on one knee. To her.)* Yamba...? Will you marry me? *(Yamba beams.)*

(To us.) Yamba and I are united in marriage. In a splendid tribal ceremony of the highest order. *(They dance and celebrate.)*

And thus begins my new life among the aborigines! *(Transition.)*

Chapter Eight. In which time passes and things change.

Yamba and I make a happy life for ourselves in our little grass hut.

We have a daughter together we call Blanche.

And, a year or so later, we have another, called Gladys. Bruno is very protective toward the girls.

He is like a watchful big brother.

They grow, seemingly overnight, into strong and beautiful young women.

There is a pleasing rhythm to this life.

Thoughts of England all but disappear. All is peaceful and predictable until one day, out of the blue ...

ENEMY TRIBESMEN. *(From off, war cry.)* WARRA HOO OOO!

LOUIS. We are attacked!

A neighboring tribe declares war!

We are forced to awaken from our lulling complacency and defend ourselves!

But there is a problem.

Gunda, our leader, is too old and feeble to take us into battle. A new war chief must be chosen. *(The tribesmen mumble in deliberation.)*

Me? But I am a man of peace, unschooled in the ways of warfare! *(To himself.)* I must come up with a strategy. What can our modest forces do to instill fear in the hearts of our enemy? We need to *appear* more powerful than we actually are.

(A beat.) I know!

I command that all of my men ... wear stilts! *(Louis and the Tribesmen, on stilts with bows and arrows, engage in battle.)*

TRIBESMEN. WARRA HOO OOO!!! *(Etc.)*

LOUIS. The enemy sees the height of our forces and thinks we are a tribe of giants!

They recoil in fear and surrender their spears!

I am hailed as a great warrior! *(The tribesmen cheer. Silence.)*

Alas, the celebration is short-lived.

This is the sad part.

The saddest part of my story you will hear.

My beloved Bruno — yes — my devoted canine friend, at this point very old and very tired, goes to sleep one night and simply never wakes up. *(To Bruno's grave.)* Goodbye, Bruno.

I would never have survived without you.

Goodbye, dear friend. *(To us.)* With Bruno gone, something inside me changes.

My heart is no longer here. *(Sunset. Louis looks off into the horizon distractedly. Yamba approaches.)*

YAMBA. Louis?

LOUIS. *(To her.)* Hm?

YAMBA. You look like you're half a world away.

LOUIS. I'm sorry.

YAMBA. You're thinking about your home, aren't you?

LOUIS. Yes.

YAMBA. Why don't we go there?

LOUIS. What?

YAMBA. I want to take you there. Back to London. You took *me* home all those many years ago. Now I want to return the favor.

LOUIS. But what about our dear girls?

What about dear Blanche and Gladys?

YAMBA. They have families of their own now. They don't need us the way they did when they were small. Let's go.

LOUIS. *(To us.)* So we do!

The tribe builds us a boat.

They bid us farewell.

We kiss our girls goodbye and we're off! *(The Tribe sees them off.)*

This journey is an ordeal. Terrible weather.

Treacherous seas. Seasickness. Mosquitoes. Sharks.

We endure months of this, when one night, Yamba makes a depressing discovery. *(Yamba points to the night sky.)*

YAMBA. *(Upset.)* Oh, no...! That's our star!

LOUIS. What do you mean?

YAMBA. We're headed back to our camp!

LOUIS. You mean all this time at sea, and we've only come full circle?!

The tribe will think me a blundering idiot!

What could I possibly say to them?

They revered me! How will I ever restore their faith?

YAMBA. *(A beat.)* I have an idea. What if...? *(She whispers into his ear.)*

LOUIS. *(To us.)* We conspire ... to tell a lie. *(Their boat returns. Louis greets the tribe like a conquering hero.)*

(To them.) My fellow tribesmen!

Yamba and I missed you so much ...

I insisted we turn back and come home!

(The tribe cheers. To us:) We are accepted back into society, but something is wrong.

Our misadventure proves one thing to me and something entirely different to Yamba: I long for England more than ever before, and she appreciates her life here just as it is. *(To Yamba.)* Yamba?

YAMBA. I know. Do what you must.

LOUIS. *(To us.)* And so I say farewell — once again and for all time — to my adopted people, to dear Blanche and sweet Gladys and to the most precious one of all, my Yamba. *(They kiss and part. Transition.)*

Chapter Nine. In which I set out due west, this time on foot, for points unknown. *(He trudges. Day into night into day.)*

I trek miles a day on rough terrain, on calloused feet, through tall grasses and deserts.

Miles and miles a day, through pitch-dark night and scorching sun, with a single thought reverberating in my head:

Home. Home. Home.

I see no one. No tribesmen. No explorers. *(Sounds of creatures.)*

Only monkeys and wombats rising in clouds and snakes and species of creatures too numerous to mention. *(He stumbles.)*

(To himself.) What's this? Boots. Discarded old boots.

(To us.) Then, a few steps further …

Tins. Toffee wrappers. Empty bottles of ale.

The first sign of civilization, and what is it?

Litter. Trash left behind in man's careless wake. *(Rowdy Australians sing.)*

(To himself.) Shhh! I must be still.

A team of Australians prospecting for gold has camped here for the night.

Food! There must be food! *(Louis rummages, finds a pastry tin.)*

What's this? *(Opens it, inhales.)* Ah! Scones! *(He eats voraciously.)*

AUSTRALIAN PROSPECTOR. Look, mates! A savage is pillaging our camp!

VARIOUS. GET HIM! KILL THE SAVAGE! SHOOT HIM! KILL HIM! *(Etc. The Prospectors are ready to shoot. Freeze. Louis, with his hands up, steps out of the action.)*

LOUIS. *(To us.)* Perhaps I should explain at this juncture how it is that I, Louis de Rougemont, am mistaken for a savage.

Imagine, if you will, my appearance.

Barefoot, filthy, half-naked but for a discreetly-placed loincloth.

Skin: sun-baked, bug-bitten and leathery.

Eyes: wild with hunger and isolation.

My knotted unruly hair goes all the way down my back, and my beard bushes out like a hawk's nest to the middle of my chest.

Is it any wonder the Australian prospectors — my would-be saviors — see me and think: savage? *(Action resumes.)*

VARIOUS. GET HIM! KILL THE SAVAGE! KILL HIM!

LOUIS. *(To the men.)* DON'T SHOOT! I BEG OF YOU!

I AM AN ENGLISHMAN!

AUSTRALIAN PROSPECTOR. The savage speaks English!

CEASE FIRE! I REPEAT! PUT DOWN YOUR GUNS! *(To Louis.)* Who are you, mate? What the hell you doin' in that get-up?

LOUIS. *(Urgently.)* My name is Louis de Rougemont!

I was shipwrecked in the Coral Sea and lived by my wits lo these many years!

AUSTRALIAN PROSPECTOR. How many?

LOUIS. That I cannot say. What year is it currently?

AUSTRALIAN PROSPECTOR. What year? Why, it's 1898.

LOUIS. 1898?! It's 1898? I set sail … in 1869.

Good Lord.

That means that I have been lost … almost *thirty* years! *(The existential reality of his adventure hits him.)*

Three decades of my life! Gone!

My entire youth! Spent! Never to be reclaimed!

Oh, woe! Oh, wretched, wretched woe! *(He breaks down in tears.)*

ANOTHER PROSPECTOR. He's mad as a hatter! Leave him.

LOUIS. No! Do not leave me here! Please, sir! I beg of you!

Take me with you! Back to civilization!

I have used up all my resources. I have nothing left.

Please, sir! If you leave me behind, I shall die! *(The Prospectors deliberate.)*

AUSTRALIAN PROSPECTOR. Alright, we'll get you as far as Brisbane. You can hop a freighter back to England from there.

LOUIS. Thank you, sir! Thank you!

(Transition. To us:) We arrive in the port city of Brisbane, Australia.

I spend the night in a local inn.

And soak — in an actual tub! — with steaming hot water and lavender soap! Ahhh! *(He does.)*

The bathwater is inky black with thirty years' worth of grime. *(He climbs out of the tub.)*

I shave my beard and cut my hair.

And climb into a soft, plush bed made with fresh linens. *(He sleeps contentedly. Transition.)*

The following morning, I work my passage on a steamship! *(A steam stack blows.)*

SHIP'S MATE. All aboard! All aboard for London, England!

VOICES. *(Variously.)* Bon voyage! Goodbye! Safe journey! *(Etc.)*

LOUIS. At long last, your humble narrator is bound for home! *(Transition.)*

Chapter Ten. Journey's End.

After weeks at sea, as the light of day begins to burn through the thick morning mist …

SHIP'S MATE. Land ho! Land ho!

LOUIS. *(Calls to Ship's Mate.)* Where? Where? I can't see! *(To us.)* The fog is so thick I see nothing beyond my own hand.

Then — presto! — like a magician's handkerchief lifted to reveal a prize:

A patch of green!

Then, mounds of it! Hills and mountains of green, and beyond them church steeples and red-roofed houses!

Am I dreaming? No, for once I am not!

It is England! I am home! *(A cacophony of urban sounds, noisier and more industrial than when Louis first heard them many years ago. Louis gets swallowed up in a crowd of bustling pedestrians.)*

(To himself.) Can this really be London?

The city I left as a sixteen-year-old youth?

(To us.) My city is a grumbling monster now, grinding its gears and spouting its smoke, all day and all night, without cease.

Factories spew coal dust and grime over every tree and cobblestone.

Atop every head, into every pore, down every throat. *(He coughs.)* While I was suspended in nature's limbo, lost in the untouched outback, something had happened.

Something inevitable yet terrifying all the same.

Something by the name of … Progress. *(A factory whistle shrieks. Transition.)*

I find my way to my mother's house as if I had last been there yesterday — not ten thousand yesterdays ago.

(Laundry hangs on a line.)

(To himself.) There it is. Just as I remember it. *(His now old mother appears with a laundry basket and proceeds to take down the wash.)*

Oh, how quaint: An old woman lives here now. *(She hums that familiar song.)*

No, wait, the old woman *is* my mother.

Look how bent she has become! How slowly she moves!

I must approach her with care so as not to startle her.

(To her, softly.) Mother?

MOTHER. Am I dead?

LOUIS. No, dear, you are not dead.

MOTHER. Are you a ghost? Have you come to take me to heaven?

LOUIS. No, it is I. Louis.

MOTHER. I had a son named Louis. He left to see the world but never came home.

LOUIS. I am he. I have returned.

MOTHER. *(Pause; chastising.) Where on earth have you been?!*

LOUIS. *(To us.)* I tell her everything. My whole amazing story.

MOTHER. What an extraordinary tale! People would be thrilled and inspired by it! You must tell your story to the world!

LOUIS. *(To her.)* But how, Mother? How can I do that?

MOTHER. *(An idea.)* I know: Look at this. *(She hands him a periodical.)*

LOUIS. *(Reads.) Wide World Magazine.*

Our motto: Truth is Stranger Than Fiction.

MOTHER. While you were gone, magazines became all the rage. Unexceptional people, it turns out, love reading about the exploits of exceptional ones. They're insatiable. Go to *Wide World*! Tell them your story! If they don't publish it, they're idiots!

LOUIS. *(With resolve.)* Alright, Mother, I will! *(To us.)* The editor is a Mr. Fitzgerald.

I go talk to him. That very day. *(A banner unfurls:* Wide World Magazine. *"Truth is Stranger Than Fiction." Louis stops Fitzgerald outside his office and follows him down the street. To him.)* Mr. Fitzgerald?

FITZGERALD. Yes?

LOUIS. My name is Louis de Rougemont and I —

FITZGERALD. Step aside. I am a vitally important man.

LOUIS. Yes, sir, I'm sure you are, sir, but I have the most extraordinary story to tell.

FITZGERALD. You and everyone else.

LOUIS. But, sir, my story is truly amazing! The most amazing story a man has ever lived to tell!

FITZGERALD. No doubt. Put it in writing. *(Fitzgerald goes. Louis types frantically. The typewriter dings with each shift of its carriage.)*

LOUIS. *(To us.)* And so, for the next several days and nights — with little pause for food or sleep — my story pours out of me in torrents of words and images …

My fateful encounter with Captain Jensen … *(Ding.)* Bruno and the pearl-divers … *(Ding.)* the giant octopus and the precious black pearls … *(Ding.)* the terrible storm and the devastating shipwreck … *(Ding.)* my years on the island … *(Ding.)* rescuing Yamba and living among the aborigines and becoming a chief and … *(Fitzgerald reads the manuscript with mounting excitement.)*

FITZGERALD. Why, this *is* amazing stuff! Breathtaking! Fantastic!

LOUIS. So you like it, then?

FITZGERALD. Like it?! I love it! It has a bit of everything! Adventure! Romance! Suspense! I'm going to publish it! In ten weekly installments, starting next week!

LOUIS. How wonderful, sir! Thank you! Thank you! *(Louis embraces Fitzgerald, who recoils.)*

FITZGERALD. No hugging.

LOUIS. Sorry.

FITZGERALD. Now, what it needs is a smart title. One that grabs the public by its throat and doesn't let go. Let's think … *(They pace and think.)*

LOUIS. How about "My Story by Louis de Rougemont"?

FITZGERALD. Too bland. It's got to be something sensational, that catches the eye and quickens the pulse. Think again. *(They pace again.)*

LOUIS. "My Thirty Years in the Australian Outback"?

FITZGERALD. No, no, no. Too academic. The object is to sell magazines! *(They pace some more.)*

LOUIS. Ah ha! I've got it!

FITZGERALD. No, *I've* got it! *Shipwrecked! The Amazing Adventures of Louis de Rougemont (As Told by Himself)!* *(A musical flourish.)*

LOUIS. Perfect! *(A Newsboy hawks copies of* Wide World *to a growing number of pedestrians.)*

NEWSBOY. *Wide World*! Get your *Wide World*! "Truth is stranger than fiction!" "Shipwrecked! Amazing True-Life Adventures of a Castaway!" Lived among cannibals! Survived thirty years in Outback! Read all about it! *(To a pedestrian.)* Wide World, mister?

PEDESTRIAN. Yeah, gimme one of those.

NEWSBOY. Here you go, sir.

ANOTHER PEDESTRIAN. I'll take one, boy.

YET ANOTHER PEDESTRIAN. I'll take two. One for my nephew.

VARIOUS. Give me one. — Me, too. — And me.

LOUIS. *(To us.)* The series proves to be so popular … *(The newsboy runs out of copies.)*

NEWSBOY. Sorry, mister. I'm all out.

MAN. Rats! Now I want it even more! *(The disappointed man walks off.)*

LOUIS. Demand is so great, the second week's printing is increased from ten thousand copies to twenty thousand!

By the third week: *fifty* thousand!

I am the man of the moment! The talk of the town! *(A parlor. Harpsichord music. Proper English society ladies in bonnets having tea.)*

SOCIETY LADY #1. The valor of this man!

SOCIETY LADY #2. The hardship!

SOCIETY LADY #1. The adversity!

SOCIETY LADY #2. I was quite moved when he fell in love with that aborigine girl.

SOCIETY LADY #1. Mm. Yes.

SOCIETY LADY #2. Yamba, I believe her name was.

SOCIETY LADY #1. Yes, Yamba! That dear, dear savage.

SOCIETY LADY #2. Mm. Yes. Quite. *(They sip their tea. Transition.)*

LOUIS. Week number six: Circulation: two hundred thousand!

Not an extra copy to be found in all of London!

My likeness appears everywhere.

I can no longer go for a stroll without being recognized. *(He's stopped by pedestrians.)*

PEDESTRIAN. Look! It's Louis de Rougemont! The famous castaway! *(Pedestrians, including a boy, Albert, and Albert's mother, applaud.)*

VARIOUS PEDESTRIANS. Bravo, sir! — Bravo! — Well done! *(Etc.)*

LOUIS. *(To them.)* Thank you, thank you, one and all. *(To us.)* I am loved! Admired! Celebrated wherever I go!

ALBERT'S MOTHER. *(To Louis, flirtatiously.)* You are quite the hero in *our* household, Mr. de Rougemont, quite the hero indeed!

LOUIS. Why, thank you, madam, you are too kind.

ALBERT'S MOTHER. Would you mind signing my little boy's copy of *Wide World*?

ALBERT. *(Embarrassed.)* Mother …

ALBERT'S MOTHER. *(Whispers to Louis.)* He's too shy to ask you himself.

LOUIS. I'd be delighted. And what is your name, little boy?

ALBERT. Albert.

LOUIS. Albert. What a mighty fine name! Do you ever dream of traveling to faraway places, Albert?

ALBERT. Oh, yes, sir, just like you!

LOUIS. Just like me, eh? What a fine lad. *(Inscribes the magazine.)* "To Albert ... May your life be an amazing adventure! Intrepidly yours, Louis de Rougemont." There you go, son. *(Hands it to Albert, who is thrilled.)*

ALBERT. Thank you, mister!

LOUIS. Albert — wait: I want you to have this. *(Louis takes the toy boat he had as a child out of his pocket.)*

ALBERT. May I have it, Mother, may I?

ALBERT'S MOTHER. No, Albert, you mustn't. *(To Louis.)* You are far too generous, sir.

LOUIS. Do let him accept it. Every child must nourish his dreams.

ALBERT. Please, Mum? Please? Please?

ALBERT'S MOTHER. *(Pause.)* All right. Very well. Say thank you, Albert.

ALBERT. Thank you, Mr. de Rougemont! You're the best! *(They go. Fitzgerald pops a champagne cork, pours two glasses.)*

FITZGERALD. Cheers, Louis! Circulation is up — to half a million!

LOUIS. Half a million?! *(To us.)* My God! I am rich! Richer than I ever imagined!

I am more than rich, I am a phenomenon!

I am immortalized in a life-size wax effigy and displayed at Madame Tussaud's! *(He strikes a pose.)*

My story is a sensation all over the world!

Translated into dozens of languages! *(Fitzgerald makes a pile of books.)*

FITZGERALD. *(Simultaneously with Louis.)* French, Italian, Spanish, German, Dutch ...

(Sotto voce.) Danish, Swahili, Swedish, Turkish, Icelandic, Greek ...

LOUIS. *(Simultaneously with Fitzgerald.)* My worldwide fame at its peak, I am summoned before Her Majesty Queen Victoria.

(Fanfare. Louis bows before Queen Victoria. To the queen:) Your Majesty.

QUEEN. For extraordinary valor in the face of seemingly insurmountable hardship and the constant threat of death at the hands of savages, we bestow upon you the honor of Member of the Order of the British Empire. *(She drapes a pendant around his neck. Music. Spectators applaud.)*

VARIOUS. Hear, hear!

LOUIS. *(To us.)* The Queen and I stroll through the topiary at Windsor Castle.

QUEEN. Tell us, Mr. de Rougemont, is it true you rode sea turtles for amusement?

LOUIS. *(To her.)* Why, yes, Your Majesty, indeed I did.

QUEEN. Tell us about that. We are most intrigued.

LOUIS. Well, ma'am, shortly after I was marooned on a remote island in the Coral Sea ... *(To us.)* The queen is so enthralled by the tale I tell, she invites me to address the Royal Geographic Society! *(A drop unfurls: the Royal Geographic Society.)*

The most prestigious such organization in all the land!

World-renowned naturalists, scientists, and zoologists come from all over to hear *me* tell *my* story!

Me! Little Louis de Rougemont!

A sickly shut-in from the wrong side of the Thames!

It is the proudest moment of my life! *(To the assembled Experts.)* And *that,* ladies and gentlemen, is where my amazing story ends! *(Pause.)* Thank you very much. *(The experts applaud, tepidly.)*

I have time for a few questions. *(Hands shoot up, and calls of "Sir!" Louis calls on the Turtle Expert.)* Yes? *(The Turtle Expert stands.)*

TURTLE EXPERT. Sir Sheldon Hardwicke, of the Liverpudlian Herpetologic College.

LOUIS. How do you do?

TURTLE EXPERT. You say you rode on the backs of sea turtles to pass the time.

LOUIS. Why, yes, sir, that is correct. As a matter of fact, just the other day, while strolling with Her Majesty —

TURTLE EXPERT. I believe you described how you were able to steer these turtles to go left or right by poking them gently in the appropriate eye? Is that right?

LOUIS. Yes. It was really quite remarkable.

TURTLE EXPERT. I'm sure. Forgive my impudence, sir ... But I have personally caught and handled *thousands* of sea turtles in my day and *not once* did I witness a turtle tolerate being touched anywhere on his body, let alone being poked in his eyes! In fact, if a man were to sit on a turtle, it would sink, straight down like a stone! *(Uproar.)*

LOUIS. *(Above the clamor.)* Not true, sir, not true!

Have you ever been on the back of a turtle?

TURTLE EXPERT. Of course I have.

LOUIS. In deep water?

TURTLE EXPERT. Well, no, not in deep water, but in shallow, certainly.

LOUIS. Not in deep water?! Then how can you contradict me, sir, if you have never tried it under such conditions?!

TURTLE EXPERT. I can contradict you, sir, because your assertion is so preposterous, it calls into question every single claim in your fantastic — indeed, unbelievable — tale! *(Uproar. An Octopus Expert leaps to his feet.)*

OCTOPUS EXPERT. Dr. Anatole Sebastian, East Anglia Oceanographic Institute. The world's foremost expert on the octopus. You say a shipmate of yours fell victim to a giant octopus?

LOUIS. Yes, sir, quite horrific it was, too. I feared it would lash out and ensnare me as well but its grasp missed me by mere inches.

HECKLER. What a shame nature failed to provide an additional foot! *(Derisive laughter.)*

OCTOPUS EXPERT. I must say: The octopus you describe, Mr. de Rougemont, possesses the anatomy and appearance of a creature that is certainly a revelation to *me!* In my twenty-five years of nautical experience in the Pacific … *(Pause for effect.)* never have I *seen* such an octopus! *(An uproar!)*

LOUIS. *(Above the din.)* But, sir, hear me out! Isn't it possible that I am the first person ever to lay eyes on such a creature?!

VARIOUS. — Nonsense!

— Absurd!

— Why, that's the most ridiculous thing I ever heard! *(Etc. A Wombat Expert stands.)*

WOMBAT EXPERT. Trevor Denniston, London Zoo. The world's leading authority on the wombat and all things wombat. *(An engraved illustration of a wombat is presented. The expert uses a pointer.)* The wombat is a species of marsupial, *genus* Vombatidae, native to Australia, about the size of a badger. The wombat is a *burrowing* animal. A root feeder that *stays close to the ground.* And yet Monsieur de Rougemont claims to have seen them, and I quote: "rising through the clouds" as if they were winged creatures! Well, let us say that that would make his adventures *truly* "amazing"! *(Laughs of derision, murmurs of agreement.)*

LOUIS. *(Over the uproar.)* Please! If I may respond! Do show me the courtesy! *(The uproar dies down.)* You are quite right, sir. I did indeed call them "wombats" —

VARIOUS. — Ah ah!

— He admits it! *(Etc.)*

LOUIS. But clearly what I *meant* was "flying squirrels."

WOMBAT EXPERT. How is it possible to confuse a wombat with a flying squirrel?! It simply isn't possible!

LOUIS. I was in error! I am only human! I concede the mistake! *(More clamor. A map of Australia is presented. A Map Maker stands.)*

MAP MAKER. *(Above the clamor.)* Point on the map, sir! Show us the exact location of the pearls you say you buried!

VOICES. *(Variously.)* Yeah! Show us! Show us, de Rougemont! *(Etc.)*

LOUIS. Sir, I would like very much to oblige ... but alas I cannot.

MAP MAKER. Cannot? What do you mean you cannot?!

HECKLER. He *says* he cannot, but the truth is *there* IS *no such place,* IS there, de Rougemont?!

LOUIS. I am sworn to secrecy! I have enlisted a syndicate for the express purpose of returning to the outback to claim the treasures I left behind!

HECKLER. Who are these people you enlisted? What are their names?

LOUIS. Their names? I ... don't remember their names.

HECKLER. Don't remember their names?!

LOUIS. Forgive me. My memory is not what it once was.

HECKLER. If that is so, why should we trust *any*thing you have to say?!

HECKLER #2. What are you hiding!? Surely you are hiding from the truth! *(Uproar.)*

LOUIS. *(Above the din.)* Mr. Kipling — the great Rudyard Kipling — dubbed it the book of the century! Who will take Mr. Kipling to task?! Who among you?!

VARIOUS. Liar! Liar! Prevaricator! *(Etc. Sounds of derision. Heckling.)*

LOUIS. Please! You must believe me! I am a man of my word!

SECOND MAN. Scoundrel!

ANOTHER MAN. CHARLATAN! *(Pause.)*

LOUIS. *(To us.)* Reporters are dispatched to uncover whatever libelous piece of filth they can get their dirty hands on.

REPORTER #2. Truth is indeed stranger than fiction. Never has that adage been more fitting than in the curious case of Louis de Rougemont.

LOUIS. *(Sarcastically.)* Curious, indeed.

REPORTER #1. He has in fact led a colorful life — but not the life described so vividly in the pages of *Wide World Magazine.*

LOUIS. What?!

REPORTER #2. Yes, he was a sickly child who was cared for by his mother, and his father *was* largely absent. But it wasn't because father was off doing business in exotic places, it was because he was a drunkard who died in debtors' prison!

LOUIS. *(To the Reporter.)* That is not entirely true!

REPORTER #1. The man who calls himself de Rougemont did not leave home at seventeen, rather his mentally imbalanced mother *threw* him out!

LOUIS. That is an affront! My mother was a saint!

REPORTER #2. He settled in London for a time, where he worked in various households as a butler and jack-of-all-trades.

REPORTER #1. It is around this time that we lose track of our subject's whereabouts. He *may* have embarked on a pearling expedition.

LOUIS. *(To us.)* Ah ha!

REPORTER #2. He may even have been shipwrecked.

LOUIS. See?! I knew I'd be vindicated.

REPORTER #1. It is possible also that said gentleman was marooned on a tiny island in one of the archipelagos off New Guinea.

LOUIS. There you go! New Guinea! That's right!

REPORTER #2. *However,* IF such a marooning took place … he could not have gone missing *more than three years.*

LOUIS. *Three* years?

REPORTER #2. For at that time, we are able to document the rescue of a lone, half-crazed castaway by an Australian trawler. The madman was brought to Sydney where he later married — *(A light comes up on Louis' wife, a harridan, looking at a picture handed her by the reporter.)*

LOUIS' WIFE. That's 'im all right, 'e ran out on me, the no-good, rotten — *(The light on her goes off.)*

REPORTER #2. — and had two daughters named — yes: Blanche and Gladys.

REPORTER #1. For the next several years he held a variety of odd jobs.

REPORTER #2. Spirit photographer.

REPORTER #1. Faith healer.

REPORTER #2. Inventor of useless contraptions.

REPORTER #1. The man who calls himself de Rougemont, deserted his wife and daughters in Sydney and returned to London.

46

REPORTER #2. There he spent countless hours in the Reading Room of the British Library concocting his fantastic story. *(A librarian holding a pile of books identifies a picture.)*

LIBRARIAN. Yes, that's him! That's the man!

REPORTER #2. *(To her.)* Are you certain?

LIBRARIAN. Quite certain. He requested every last book we had on the Australian outback. Oh, yes: As I recall, he had a particular fascination for the aborigines.

REPORTER #2. It is the sober conclusion of this investigation that de Rougemont, took the three years he was unaccounted for and simply added a zero to the truth. *(Louis is alone.)*

LOUIS. *(To us.)* Truth? What *is* truth?

Can one *hold* it? Is it rock? Is it bone?

If I am guilty of anything it is of dabbing a few spots of color on the drab canvas of life. *(A newsboy enters.)*

NEWSBOY. *Chronicle!* Get your *Daily Chronicle!* De Rougemont exposed as fraud! *(To Louis.)* Paper, mister?

LOUIS. *(To Newsboy.)* No, thanks. *(To us.)* My life takes an ugly turn.

I am mocked. Ridiculed. Reviled. *(Harpsichord music. The society ladies have another tea.)*

SOCIETY LADY #1. That vile, awful man!

SOCIETY LADY #2. The man is a fool!

SOCIETY LADY #1. Ah, but who's the bigger fool? Is he, or are we for believing him?

SOCIETY LADY #2. Hm. Yes. Quite. *(They sip their tea.)*

LOUIS. My shame takes all kinds of shape. *(He encounters Albert, who weeps.)*

LOUIS. *(To Albert.)* Little boy. What is your name?

ALBERT. It's Albert, sir. Remember me?

LOUIS. My goodness! Albert! Of course, I remember you.

Why are you crying, son? Why the tears?

ALBERT. It's you, sir.

LOUIS. I?

ALBERT. You lied to me! I believed everything you said! You were my hero! *(Albert throws the toy boat to the ground and runs away.)*

LOUIS. *(Calls to him.)* Albert! Come back! Don't leave me! *(Dr. Leopold steps forward.)*

DR. LEOPOLD. *(Viennese accent.)* Ladies and gentlemen. My name is Leopold. Dr. Hans Leopold of Vienna, Austria. I am an alienist by profession.

Upon close, textual analysis, I found that certain passages and events in the subject's autobiography seemed to reflect — perhaps unconsciously — the experiences and inventions of writers who came before him. *(Mother's lullaby theme is heard.)* It is likely that the books his mother read to him as a boy came back to him as actual personal experiences, and he made those adventures his own. He took his uneventful life of failure and reinvented it as one filled with spectacle and triumph. Louis de Rougemont did *not* deliberately delude his public, ladies and gentlemen, but rather ... *he himself is deluded!* My diagnosis? *(Pause.)* Delusions of grandeur. *(Dr. Leopold goes. Louis seems to have aged before our eyes.)*

LOUIS. *(To himself, shaken.)* Deluded? Me? I am not deluded.

Am I? *(He seems lost, as if he's forgotten his lines. The Players are concerned.)*

PLAYER #1. *(Sotto; feeds his line.)* "Time goes by."

LOUIS. *(Pause. Then to her, vaguely.)* Hm? *(The house lights come up.)*

PLAYER #1. *(Sotto.)* "Time goes by. The firestorm ... " See? *(She points within the script. Player #2 brings him a cup of water.)*

LOUIS. Oh. Thank you.

PLAYER #1. *(Whispers.)* Mr. de Rougemont? Are you alright? Do you feel well enough to go on?

LOUIS. Yes, yes. I'm fine. Thank you. You are most kind. *(The Players go. House lights down. Resumes, to us:)* Time goes by. The firestorm dies down.

Soon Louis de Rougemont is a forgotten man. *(A pedestrian walks past him.)*

PEDESTRIAN. Louis *who?*

LOUIS. I fall on hard times.

I lose whatever riches my fame had brought me.

All my money and possessions go to lawyers who defend my honor. Unsuccessfully. *(A Lawyer wearing a white wig, removes the pendant from around Louis' neck ...)*

LAWYER. *(Curtly.)* Thank you. *(... and replaces it with a crudely printed sign that reads: I WILL TELL MY STORY FOR MONEY.)*

LOUIS. I am penniless.

I live by my wits on the streets of London. *(To a young man.)* Story? Story, boy?

I have a fantastic story to tell! An amazing adventure!

YOUNG MAN. Ah, go away, you old crank. *(A woman holding an infant goes by.)*

LOUIS. *(To the Woman.)* Story? Story, m'am? A penny for my story?

(The woman shuns him. To us:) The public, with the bloodthirsty glee of cannibals feasting on human flesh, moves on to devour its next victim.

And its next, and the one after that.

There are and there shall always be man-made gods the *hoi polloi* eagerly creates and then just as eagerly destroys.

I am merely one in a long illustrious line. *(Transition.)*

I am old now.

I have but one amazing adventure yet to come.

The adventure that comes to all living things.

What does a man leave behind but his name and the stories he told? All else is dust.

I am prepared to take my leave, and dwell for eternity among the ignominious, but ... before I bid you farewell, I wish to make — here and now — one last attempt to restore my good name.

Gentle ladies and kind men ...

The *piece de resistance* of this evening's entertainment! *(A tank of water is unveiled, and in it a sea turtle.)*

Behold! A tank of water!

Observe!

This decrepit laughing-stock will now mount and ride a sea turtle!

Impossible, you say?

A man cannot ride a sea turtle for his amusement?

Anyone who claims as much must be a liar?

Or a charlatan? Or a fool?

We shall see about *that* ... *(Louis disrobes, revealing a bathing costume. He responds to a man in the audience.)*

Do you snicker, sir?

At what? The spectacle of a ridiculous old man?

You dast not snicker at me, sir.

You may be old one day, too, if you're fortunate.

You may one day be an old man fighting for his life. *(He climbs into the tank and mounts the turtle.)*

(To us.) Observe!

Ever so gingerly I hoist myself onto his gnarly shell as if it is a well-worn saddle.

My legs around either side.

Observe, ladies and gentlemen:
I am seated upon the turtle!
Does the reptile reject me?
No, he does not.
Does he roll over and toss me off?
No.
Does he sink like a stone?
Most decidedly not!
No, he contentedly floats along the surface with me upon him!
When I wish to turn left, I poke him gently in his right eye.
When I wish to go right, I poke his left.
Ha ha! How wonderful!
Observe! all you detractors and doubters out there who relished my undoing.
Who picked every nit in the hopes of unraveling the tapestry of my amazing adventure.
Observe! all you skeptics and anti-dreamers!
You small-minded logicians and earthbound star-gazers!
Believe what you will about me.
But seeing is believing, is it not?
Look at me! Look at me, world! Look at Louis now!
Good night, dear ones great and small!
Sweet dreams!
(Laughing joyfully, he rides the sea turtle.)
Whheeeeeeeeee! (Lights fade to black.)

End of Play

AFTERWORD
AN EMPTY STAGE IN HALF-LIGHT

More than a quarter century ago, the critic Robert Hughes called the public's response to modern art "the shock of the new." The role of art was to stimulate ideas, provoke thought, challenge ways of seeing. Today we are experiencing a different, troubling phenomenon: a popular culture that embraces the comfort of the familiar.

Americans discovered the hard way that we don't like surprises. Now that fear and uncertainty have taken permanent residence, people are unnerved by ambiguity in all aspects of life. They look for reassurance in rituals that are concrete and predictable.

Newness is suspect. Constancy is rewarded. The consumer will go to McDonald's expressly for its Big Mac, or to DQ for its Blizzard, go home satisfied, and make repeated return visits for the same reliable product. The fast-food culture now extends to the entertainment industry. Here the consumer has a pretty good idea what he's going to see before he sees it, and seems to prefer it that way. How else do we explain the proliferation of stage adaptations of movies on stage and the domination of the franchise in the world of motion pictures?

Movie franchises promise plotlines that rely on tried and true formulas, and reunions with characters who, over time, seem like old friends. There is little surprise and no real jeopardy because these heroes are invincible: Bourne/Bond will surely endure because too much rides on his appearing in the next installment.

Serials, of course, are nothing new; they have been a part of the movie-going tradition from the earliest days of the medium but nowadays they have become industries unto themselves. They are pre-sold products with instant name recognition and built-in audiences; and the public, pressed to put their limited leisure time and entertainment dollars to good use, with as little risk as possible, will invariably choose to spend their time and money on the sure thing.

Can we blame them? A night at the movies for a family of four, once you factor in parking, popcorn and that personal liter of Coke, could easily approach a hundred dollars; a night on Broadway for the same foursome could cost more than five times that. Is it any wonder consumers want to know what their buck will get them before they plunk it down at the box office?

Today's theatergoing audiences can hum the "score" of *Jersey Boys*,

51

the Four Seasons musical, before they enter the theater; they can anticipate the best lines from *Legally Blonde: The Musical*, and know Celie's fate before the curtain comes up on *The Color Purple*. They howled at their favorite shtick in Mel Brooks' *The Producers* and are likely to do the same with his *Young Frankenstein*. The good financial news is that Broadway had a record-breaking year, but you know we've turned some kind of cultural corner when the once-subversive Monty Python can be re-packaged for mainstream audiences as a benign greatest-hits extravaganza. (A notable exception to this recycling trend in musicals is the fresh and challenging *Spring Awakening*, whose source is a dark, nineteenth-century text by Frank Wedekind, unknown to but a handful of its potential audience.)

Even non-musicals derived from popular films have made their way to the commercial stage: *The Graduate* gave certain aging actresses a chance to show they still looked good with their clothes off (and sold a surprising number of tickets to the curious); and now *Guess Who's Coming to Dinner?*, the soothing racial comedy-drama from the sixties, is also headed for Broadway.

Pity the poor dramatist living in an age in which movies have opening dates before they have scripts, television eschews scripts altogether in favor of contrived "reality" programs, and Broadway has been reduced to a theme park where theatergoers can see some of their favorite movies performed live.

Dire pronouncements about the moribund state of the American theater have been made for decades but, like the formerly remote concept of global warming, there is every indication that its demise has finally come. The audience for "serious" theater (straight plays) is dwindling. The subscriber base — the life force of not-for-profit theaters for half a century — is literally dying, and the next generation is not filling their seats. That group, the aging boomer, is too consumed by the demands of their careers, putting their kids through school, and caring for their failing elders (those vanishing subscribers) to make theatergoing the vital part of their lives it was for their parents.

Young people have so many options at their fingertips that the plight of the theatre must seem almost quaint to them, certainly irrelevant. How can theater, with its technologic limitations, possibly compete with the vast arsenal of entertainment available to them?

Spectacular computer-generated graphics have made imagination redundant. The creative energy expended is that of the artist;

the viewer is made utterly passive. Nothing is required of him but to sit back and receive a seemingly endless barrage of fantastic images, a sensory assault that comes at him so quickly he barely has a chance to sort them out. The collateral damage of all his technology is the atrophy of imagination. Audiences are losing their ability to supply imagery of their own design and are becoming increasingly concrete in their thinking.

I was at the movies recently, in the company of two media-savvy teenagers. During the numbing onslaught of trailers (I can't tell you what they were for, they've all melded in my memory as one noisy, ugly, ultra-violent, would-be blockbuster), a special effect flashed by: cars flipping through the air, crashing, and exploding into a fireball, that sort of thing. My companions were unimpressed.

"Oh, man, that looks so fake," one said, and they both laughed.

Their derision saddened me. Have we so inundated our children with technical wizardry that they've lost their capacity for wonder? Have computer-generated armies of thousands and intergalactic conflagrations become so commonplace that they feel they can dismiss an effect if it fails to meet their high standard? I think we've all lost something precious when effects that might have thrilled earlier generations to death are derided by today's young pseudo-sophisticates as feeble attempts.

I watched a lot of television when I was young, and remember being enthralled by series like *Star Trek* and *I, Claudius*. I went willingly to wherever they took me, whether it was outer space or ancient Rome, and never stopped to weigh their production values. When I watched those programs again recently I was amazed by how endearingly cheesy they were. Their sound-stage origins were barely disguised but I don't remember ever remarking on their artifice. I was too invested in the characters and the stories being told to notice, let alone care.

The oral tradition of storytelling was perhaps best exemplified by the radio play. Stories came to life through sound, music, voice, descriptive language. The listener's imagination did the rest.

Orson Welles' Mercury Theatre radio production of H.G. Wells' *War of the Worlds* famously terrified its audience into thinking that a Martian invasion had taken place in Grovers Mill, New Jersey. (It was so persuasive that, according to family lore, my Aunt Pauline wailed,

"And we just bought new furniture!") Contemporary listeners would probably find the performance too stagy to be believed, but its 1938 audience, still reeling from the Depression, readily suspended their disbelief. It was all too plausible that their tenuous lives could be taken away from them, even by marauding Martians. Welles and company knew the seductive power of a good story and innately understood the potential of electronic media as theater on a grand scale.

The magic of theater is its power to astonish, but astonishment can occur only if the audience is willing to suspend its disbelief. How are we expected to astonish young people who have seen everything imaginable, on screens of all description, since they were born?

We need to build a new tradition of theatergoing if the theater is to survive. The challenge is to invite this potential audience in to the theater, to entertain and move them and make them laugh. If we do our job well, they'll come again and keep coming, and one day bring *their* children. If we don't, if we bore or alienate them, we could lose them forever.

How often have you gone to a play, even a highly touted one, only to be bored? You'll forgive a bad movie, which can be amusing even in its badness, but sitting through a bad or tedious play can be punishing. You're trapped, at least until intermission, and you resent being trapped. You sit there festering about all the money you spent, and the damn critics who said this was good, and the episode of *Mad Men* you could have been watching on TiVo for free in your own living room.

My aim was to capture the attention of the hidden child in everyone in my audience. I wanted to write a play that would make no attempt to replicate on stage what television and movies do but would instead celebrate the uniqueness of theater. My impulse was to strip away the trappings of spectacle and get back to what theater does best: tell stories that reflect our world or create new ones; that can enlighten, amuse, transport, make you forget, or force you to remember.

I set out to tell a ripping good yarn, the sort of narrative that captivated me when I was a boy, that I think enthralled all of us. For my subject, I was drawn to a story about the very nature of storytelling.

A few years ago, while researching a movie I was writing about a Holocaust survivor-pretender, I read a book called *Impostors: Six Kinds of Liar* by Sarah Burton. In it was the curious true-life tale of Louis de Rougemont, a man whose exploits transfixed the Victorian public. Louis claimed to have survived, among many other travails, a spectacular shipwreck in the South Seas, an attack by a giant octopus, and thirty years among a tribe of cannibals. His serialized story made him famous, a celebrity author not unlike the Oprah Winfrey–anointed James Frey, whose veracity (like Frey's) was ultimately called into question. Louis' story stayed with me. In fact, the Frey controversy reawakened my interest in it. (Frey wrote *A Million Little Pieces*, a memoir that turned out to be significantly fabricated, for which Frey was publicly dressed down by his erstwhile patroness.) The story of Louis de Rougemont, his rise and fall, had all the elements of a classic picaresque: A young man leaves home to find himself, goes on a long and unpredictable journey, survives extraordinary events, finds fame, tells lies. In it I saw the potential for a purely theatrical play about the power of imagination.

Whenever I start contemplating a new play, I re-read one of my favorites, Thornton Wilder's *Our Town*. Revisiting Grovers Corners has become a ritual of mine, like cleansing one's palette with sherbet between courses. Every time I read it, I make new discoveries. For this new play — *Shipwrecked! An Entertainment* — *The Amazing Adventures of Louis de Rougemont (As Told by Himself)* — I found inspiration in its very first words:

"No curtain.

No scenery.

The audience, arriving, sees an empty stage in half-light."

—Donald Margulies

This essay originally appeared in the Los Angeles Times *on September 23, 2007. Reprinted with permission.*

PROPERTY LIST

Note
Gramophone
Racks of clothing, props, steamer trunks
Blanket
Stuffed animal (dog)
Hot scone
Book, toy boat
Laundry, nightshirt, laundry basket
Book, cash, purse
Pointer
Pearls
Jars of pearls
Broken hand mirror
Coconut shell
Headdress
Delicacies in baskets
Stilts, bows and arrows
Pastry tin
Periodical
Typewriter, paper
Manuscript
Newspapers
Tea things
Champagne bottle, two glasses
OBE medal pendant
Photo
Pile of books
Cup of water
Neck sign
Baby

SOUND EFFECTS

Scratchy gramophone recording of fanfare
Children singing and playing in distance
Mother's lullaby theme
Raging storm
City and marketplace sounds
Wind chimes
Sailor's sea shanty
Ominous music
Wind, rumble of thunder
Lightning
Tempest
Sibilant whoosh
Dog howling
Thunder, lightning, rain
Smack of giant wave
Snapping break and fall of mast
Seagulls
Owls, waves, wombats
Pluck of violin string
Volcano rumble
Rowdy Australians singing
Steamboat whistle
Factory whistle
Typing
Typewriter return "ding"
Harpsichord music
Pop of champagne bottle
Fanfare

NEW PLAYS

★ **GUARDIANS by Peter Morris.** In this unflinching look at war, a disgraced American soldier discloses the truth about Abu Ghraib prison, and a clever English journalist reveals how he faked a similar story for the London tabloids. "Compelling, sympathetic and powerful." –*NY Times.* "Sends you into a state of moral turbulence." –*Sunday Times (UK).* "Nothing short of remarkable." –*Village Voice.* [1M, 1W] ISBN: 978-0-8222-2177-7

★ **BLUE DOOR by Tanya Barfield.** Three generations of men (all played by one actor), from slavery through Black Power, challenge Lewis, a tenured professor of mathematics, to embark on a journey combining past and present. "A teasing flare for words." –*Village Voice.* "Unfailingly thought-provoking." –*LA Times.* "The play moves with the speed and logic of a dream." –*Seattle Weekly.* [2M] ISBN: 978-0-8222-2209-5

★ **THE INTELLIGENT DESIGN OF JENNY CHOW by Rolin Jones.** This irreverent "techno-comedy" chronicles one brilliant woman's quest to determine her heritage and face her fears with the help of her astounding creation called Jenny Chow. "Boldly imagined." –*NY Times.* "Fantastical and funny." –*Variety.* "Harvests many laughs and finally a few tears." –*LA Times.* [3M, 3W] ISBN: 978-0-8222-2071-8

★ **SOUVENIR by Stephen Temperley.** Florence Foster Jenkins, a wealthy society eccentric, suffers under the delusion that she is a great coloratura soprano—when in fact the opposite is true. "Hilarious and deeply touching. Incredibly moving and breathtaking." –*NY Daily News.* "A sweet love letter of a play." –*NY Times.* "Wildly funny. Completely charming." –*Star-Ledger.* [1M, 1W] ISBN: 978-0-8222-2157-9

★ **ICE GLEN by Joan Ackermann.** In this touching period comedy, a beautiful poetess dwells in idyllic obscurity on a Berkshire estate with a band of unlikely cohorts. "A beautifully written story of nature and change." –*Talkin' Broadway.* "A lovely play which will leave you with a lot to think about." –*CurtainUp.* "Funny, moving and witty." –*Metroland (Boston).* [4M, 3W] ISBN: 978-0-8222-2175-3

★ **THE LAST DAYS OF JUDAS ISCARIOT by Stephen Adly Guirgis.** Set in a time-bending, darkly comic world between heaven and hell, this play reexamines the plight and fate of the New Testament's most infamous sinner. "An unforced eloquence that finds the poetry in lowdown street talk." –*NY Times.* "A real jaw-dropper." –*Variety.* "An extraordinary play." –*Guardian (UK).* [10M, 5W] ISBN: 978-0-8222-2082-4

DRAMATISTS PLAY SERVICE, INC.
440 Park Avenue South, New York, NY 10016 212-683-8960 Fax 212-213-1539
postmaster@dramatists.com www.dramatists.com

NEW PLAYS

★ **THE GREAT AMERICAN TRAILER PARK MUSICAL music and lyrics by David Nehls, book by Betsy Kelso.** Pippi, a stripper on the run, has just moved into Armadillo Acres, wreaking havoc among the tenants of Florida's most exclusive trailer park. "Adultery, strippers, murderous ex-boyfriends, Costco and the Ice Capades. Undeniable fun." *–NY Post.* "Joyful and unashamedly vulgar." *–The New Yorker.* "Sparkles with treasure." *–New York Sun.* [2M, 5W] ISBN: 978-0-8222-2137-1

★ **MATCH by Stephen Belber.** When a young Seattle couple meet a prominent New York choreographer, they are led on a fraught journey that will change their lives forever. "Uproariously funny, deeply moving, enthralling theatre." *–NY Daily News.* "Prolific laughs and ear-to-ear smiles." *–NY Magazine.* [2M, 1W] ISBN: 978-0-8222-2020-6

★ **MR. MARMALADE by Noah Haidle.** Four-year-old Lucy's imaginary friend, Mr. Marmalade, doesn't have much time for her—not to mention he has a cocaine addiction and a penchant for pornography. "Alternately hilarious and heartbreaking." *–The New Yorker.* "A mature and accomplished play." *–LA Times.* "Scathingly observant comedy." *–Miami Herald.* [4M, 2W] ISBN: 978-0-8222-2142-5

★ **MOONLIGHT AND MAGNOLIAS by Ron Hutchinson.** Three men cloister themselves as they work tirelessly to reshape a screenplay that's just not working—*Gone with the Wind.* "Consumers of vintage Hollywood insider stories will eat up Hutchinson's diverting conjecture." *–Variety.* "A lot of fun." *–NY Post.* "A Hollywood dream-factory farce." *–Chicago Sun-Times.* [3M, 1W] ISBN: 978-0-8222-2084-8

★ **THE LEARNED LADIES OF PARK AVENUE by David Grimm, translated and freely adapted from Molière's Les Femmes Savantes.** Dicky wants to marry Betty, but her mother's plan is for Betty to wed a most pompous man. "A brave, brainy and barmy revision." *–Hartford Courant.* "A rare but welcome bird in contemporary theatre." *–New Haven Register.* "Roll over Cole Porter." *–Boston Globe.* [5M, 5W] ISBN: 978-0-8222-2135-7

★ **REGRETS ONLY by Paul Rudnick.** A sparkling comedy of Manhattan manners that explores the latest topics in marriage, friendships and squandered riches. "One of the funniest quip-meisters on the planet." *–NY Times.* "Precious moments of hilarity. Devastatingly accurate political and social satire." *–BackStage.* "Great fun." *–CurtainUp.* [3M, 3W] ISBN: 978-0-8222-2223-1

DRAMATISTS PLAY SERVICE, INC.
440 Park Avenue South, New York, NY 10016 212-683-8960 Fax 212-213-1539
postmaster@dramatists.com www.dramatists.com

NEW PLAYS

★ **AFTER ASHLEY by Gina Gionfriddo.** A teenager is unwillingly thrust into the national spotlight when a family tragedy becomes talk-show fodder. "A work that virtually any audience would find accessible." –*NY Times.* "Deft characterization and caustic humor." –*NY Sun.* "A smart satirical drama." –*Variety.* [4M, 2W] ISBN: 978-0-8222-2099-2

★ **THE RUBY SUNRISE by Rinne Groff.** Twenty-five years after Ruby struggles to realize her dream of inventing the first television, her daughter faces similar battles of faith as she works to get Ruby's story told on network TV. "Measured and intelligent, optimistic yet clear-eyed." –*NY Magazine.* "Maintains an exciting sense of ingenuity." –*Village Voice.* "Sinuous theatrical flair." –*Broadway.com.* [3M, 4W] ISBN: 978-0-8222-2140-1

★ **MY NAME IS RACHEL CORRIE taken from the writings of Rachel Corrie, edited by Alan Rickman and Katharine Viner.** This solo piece tells the story of Rachel Corrie who was killed in Gaza by an Israeli bulldozer set to demolish a Palestinian home. "Heartbreaking urgency. An invigoratingly detailed portrait of a passionate idealist." –*NY Times.* "Deeply authentically human." –*USA Today.* "A stunning dramatization." –*CurtainUp.* [1W] ISBN: 978-0-8222-2222-4

★ **ALMOST, MAINE by John Cariani.** This charming midwinter night's dream of a play turns romantic clichés on their ear as it chronicles the painfully hilarious amorous adventures (and misadventures) of residents of a remote northern town that doesn't quite exist. "A whimsical approach to the joys and perils of romance." –*NY Times.* "Sweet, poignant and witty." –*NY Daily News.* "Aims for the heart by way of the funny bone." –*Star-Ledger.* [2M, 2W] ISBN: 978-0-8222-2156-2

★ **Mitch Albom's TUESDAYS WITH MORRIE by Jeffrey Hatcher and Mitch Albom, based on the book by Mitch Albom.** The true story of Brandeis University professor Morrie Schwartz and his relationship with his student Mitch Albom. "A touching, life-affirming, deeply emotional drama." –*NY Daily News.* "You'll laugh. You'll cry." –*Variety.* "Moving and powerful." –*NY Post.* [2M] ISBN: 978-0-8222-2188-3

★ **DOG SEES GOD: CONFESSIONS OF A TEENAGE BLOCKHEAD by Bert V. Royal.** An abused pianist and a pyromaniac ex-girlfriend contribute to the teen-angst of America's most hapless kid. "A welcome antidote to the notion that the *Peanuts* gang provides merely American cuteness." –*NY Times.* "Hysterically funny." –*NY Post.* "The *Peanuts* kids have finally come out of their shells." –*Time Out.* [4M, 4W] ISBN: 978-0-8222-2152-4

DRAMATISTS PLAY SERVICE, INC.
440 Park Avenue South, New York, NY 10016 212-683-8960 Fax 212-213-1539
postmaster@dramatists.com www.dramatists.com

NEW PLAYS

★ **RABBIT HOLE by David Lindsay-Abaire.** Winner of the 2007 Pulitzer Prize. Becca and Howie Corbett have everything a couple could want until a life-shattering accident turns their world upside down. "An intensely emotional examination of grief, laced with wit." *—Variety.* "A transcendent and deeply affecting new play." *—Entertainment Weekly.* "Painstakingly beautiful." *—BackStage.* [2M, 3W] ISBN: 978-0-8222-2154-8

★ **DOUBT, A Parable by John Patrick Shanley.** Winner of the 2005 Pulitzer Prize and Tony Award. Sister Aloysius, a Bronx school principal, takes matters into her own hands when she suspects the young Father Flynn of improper relations with one of the male students. "All the elements come invigoratingly together like clockwork." *—Variety.* "Passionate, exquisite, important, engrossing." *—NY Newsday.* [1M, 3W] ISBN: 978-0-8222-2219-4

★ **THE PILLOWMAN by Martin McDonagh.** In an unnamed totalitarian state, an author of horrific children's stories discovers that someone has been making his stories come true. "A blindingly bright black comedy." *—NY Times.* "McDonagh's least forgiving, bravest play." *—Variety.* "Thoroughly startling and genuinely intimidating." *—Chicago Tribune.* [4M, 5 bit parts (2M, 1W, 1 boy, 1 girl)] ISBN: 978-0-8222-2100-5

★ **GREY GARDENS book by Doug Wright, music by Scott Frankel, lyrics by Michael Korie.** The hilarious and heartbreaking story of Big Edie and Little Edie Bouvier Beale, the eccentric aunt and cousin of Jacqueline Kennedy Onassis, once bright names on the social register who became East Hampton's most notorious recluses. "An experience no passionate theatergoer should miss." *—NY Times.* "A unique and unmissable musical." *—Rolling Stone.* [4M, 3W, 2 girls] ISBN: 978-0-8222-2181-4

★ **THE LITTLE DOG LAUGHED by Douglas Carter Beane.** Mitchell Green could make it big as the hot new leading man in Hollywood if Diane, his agent, could just keep him in the closet. "Devastatingly funny." *—NY Times.* "An out-and-out delight." *—NY Daily News.* "Full of wit and wisdom." *—NY Post.* [2M, 2W] ISBN: 978-0-8222-2226-2

★ **SHINING CITY by Conor McPherson.** A guilt-ridden man reaches out to a therapist after seeing the ghost of his recently deceased wife. "Haunting, inspired and glorious." *—NY Times.* "Simply breathtaking and astonishing." *—Time Out.* "A thoughtful, artful, absorbing new drama." *—Star-Ledger.* [3M, 1W] ISBN: 978-0-8222-2187-6

DRAMATISTS PLAY SERVICE, INC.
440 Park Avenue South, New York, NY 10016 212-683-8960 Fax 212-213-1539
postmaster@dramatists.com www.dramatists.com